Low-FODMAP Diet for Beginners

Dr. Beth Ganley

Dedication

I thank my many friends and family members for their support and helpful suggestions: Kate, Rosy, Aly, Very, Dr. Rob.

I give thanks to God for the incredible energy, clarity, and support I received in bringing forth this book.

Table of Contents

Introduction

Before you started to diagnose and treat your symptoms of Irritable Bowel Syndrome (IBS) or other gastrointestinal discomforts, you had probably never heard of the low FODMAP diet. After you were diagnosed with IBS, you were probably told by your doctor to visit a nutritionist to build a personalized plan using the low FODMAP diet. However, before you did that, you scoured the internet to get an idea about what this diet entails. All of that preparation has led you here.

The low FODMAP diet will help you determine which foods are causing your symptoms, so you can diminish or eliminate the amount that you eat. It is a constructive way in learning to soothe your gut and relieve IBS symptoms naturally. Using the low FODMAP diet will make you more in touch with your body and its reactions to food, so you can gain a better relationship with your body and the food you consume.

This book will teach you all you need to know about FODMAPs, which are a distinct class of carbohydrates. Certain FODMAPs can cause sensitive individuals to have symptoms of bloating, gas, and stomach pains at varying levels, which is especially true for people who suffer from IBS. You will find that by using the low FODMAP diet methods, you will gain more control over these symptoms, and maybe even eliminate them entirely, leading you to feeling better much quicker.

This systematic method is easy to follow, although it may seem daunting at first. Though it is possible to do this diet on your own, it is also highly recommended to seek guidance of a medical practitioner and a licensed nutritionist, so you can glide more smoothly through the process. Each body is different, so this customizable diet will be a little different for each person; however, the basics stay the same.

Once you follow the method outlined in this book, you will be able to remove these troublesome high FODMAPS from your diet and will start to feel positive effects within a week. The next step would be to test each high FODMAP to determine which foods your body finds the most troublesome. Using this method, you will be able to pinpoint these foods and learn to incorporate them differently. In some cases, you will learn which food types are not good for your body at all and eliminate them from your diet.

This diet is ideal for those who suffer from diagnosed diabetes, ulcerative colitis, Crohn's disease, celiac disease, and IBS. It is also beneficial for those who are following either a dairy-free, low-fat, vegan, or vegetarian diet. For those who have occasional stomach upset or digestive issues, this method may be more detrimental as a diet, as your body can handle high FODMAPs that agitate diagnosed patients with gastrointestinal disorders.

Included, you will find a method with which to follow along and handy tips to be successful. There will be an explanation of gastrointestinal disorders, as well as some of the benefits that come with following this diet. You will get an up-to-date listing of high FODMAP foods that you will need to avoid, as well as a sample shopping list for items that are safe and low FODMAPs. There are even some money-saving tips you can use while following this diet. This book contains a week-long guide for getting started with today, which will give you daily suggestions for what to eat during your meals.

There are 101 delicious recipes in this book that are categorized in an easy-to-follow fashion, making it simple for you to find recipes for foods that you have on hand. The variety of recipes included will help you not get tired of eating the same old recipes. Each recipe will include macros, preparation, and cook time, along with a detailed and easy-to-follow set of instructions, which will make each meal simple to make, even if you are not a master chef. There are even tips for substitutions that will add variety to the included recipes. These recipes were created with a family in mind, but you can always store leftovers and divide or multiply the recipes to your personal needs.

I promise that with this book, you will become much more educated about the low FODMAP diet, foods that are high in FODMAPs, and how to customize your own eating plan to better your gut and overall health. No longer will you be revolving your life around your symptoms; instead, you will be able to enjoy your life and become much happier doing so. You will start to notice a difference in your life after a short period if you follow the steps outlined in this book, and you will find it liberating to be living your life without these debilitating symptoms.

So why delay? Make a difference today in your health. If you knew there was a chance that you could live a life without your gastrointestinal symptoms and a need for medications or surgery, why not take that opportunity? This book will be able to help you at every step of the way.

Chapter One:
What is the Low FODMAP Diet and Who Needs It?

Digestive issues, such as **Irritable Bowel Syndrome (IBS)** and other **functional gastrointestinal disorders (FGID)** like constipation, diarrhea, and bloating, can commonly be triggered by certain foods and allergies. When you eliminate these troublesome foods and slowly reintroduce them briefly back into your body, you can easily test to see what specific foods are not good for your overall health. When you follow this easy guide to the low FODMAP diet and ease it into your lifestyle, you will come to better understand these foods, so you can then eliminate them from your diet altogether and will no longer suffer from digestive issues in the future.

This is a short-term diet that lasts anywhere from two to six weeks, but what you learn will grant you lasting effects. It will also put you more in touch with your body and your overall health. You will realize these changes in your life can make you stronger, healthier, and grant you more freedom from gut-related issues.

The name of this diet derives from **FODMAP foods**, which are carbohydrates resistant to proper digestion. These foods will pass through non-sensitive individuals' digestive systems, and are known as **dietary fiber**. For those sensitive individuals, the FODMAPs are absorbed into your bloodstream, where they then travel toward where gut bacteria are in your intestines. This results in the FODMAPs being used for fuel, which creates hydrogen gas and causes an experience of digestive discomfort. They can also draw liquid into the digestive tract that could lead to diarrhea.

F ERMENTABLE
O LIGOSACCHARIDES
D ISACCHARIDES
M ONOSACCHARIDES
A ND
P OLYOLS

FODMAP stands for **Fermentable Oligo Di Monosaccharides and Polyols**.[1]

They can be broken down into four different groups:

Oligosaccharides—Garlic, onions, legumes, rye, and wheat

Disaccharides—Lactose in soft cheeses, yogurt, and milk

Monosaccharides—Fructose in Agave nectar, honey, and food sweeteners. This category also includes mangoes and figs.

---

[1] Gibson, P. R., and S. J. Shepherd. "Personal View: Food for Thought - Western Lifestyle and Susceptibility to Crohn's Disease. The FODMAP Hypothesis." Alimentary Pharmacology and Therapeutics, vol. 21, no. 12, 2005, pp. 1399–1409., doi:10.1111/j.1365-2036.2005.02506.x.

Polyols—Some low-calorie sweeteners, lychees, and blackberries.

Other common high FODMAP foods include the following:

- animal milk
- apples
- applesauce
- apricots
- artichokes
- asparagus
- baked beans
- barley
- beans
- beer
- beetroot
- Blackberries
- boysenberries
- breakfast cereal
- broccoli
- Brussel sprouts
- cabbage
- canned fruit
- Cashews
- cauliflower
- cherries
- chickpeas
- crackers
- dates
- fennel
- fortified wine
- fruit juice
- high fructose corn syrup
- ice cream
- leeks
- lentils
- maltitol
- mannitol
- most yogurts
- mushrooms
- Nectarines
- okra
- pasta
- peaches
- pears
- peas
- pistachios
- pistachios
- red kidney beans
- rye
- shallots
- sorbitol
- sour cream
- soy milk
- soybean
- tortillas
- watermelon
- wheat
- whey protein supplements
- xylitol

These types of carbs can cause digestive issues, ranging from stomach pain, gas, and bloating. As you have probably noticed from the chart, FODMAPs are present in a wide range of foods and can contain either one or several types of the above-mentioned categories. Even though it may appear overwhelming at first, we will be going over some easy-to-follow steps in the following chapters that will make it much easier for you to follow this diet. As you will see, there are various tasty and healthy alternatives that you can eat to feel better. It is also important to remember that the low FODMAP diet's purpose is not necessarily to eliminate these foods completely; the amount of it you consume just needs to be minimized significantly, which will allow you to reduce your digestive symptoms.

Who Should Follow the Low FODMAP Diet?

This is not a diet designed for every person. In fact, it is best to follow it only if you have been diagnosed with IBS or another FGID because there is harm that can come to those without major digestive issues. The principal reason to follow this diet is that FODMAPS are in most prebiotics, which help support your digestive system with healthy bacteria.[2] Based on the significant amount of research being conducted on adults who suffer from IBS, it is also suggested to get support from your doctor if you have a child suffering from IBS.

Because there are differing digestive symptoms that can occur, you need to determine whether they are harmless or more serious. There is no diagnostic test to determine if you suffer from IBS, so you need to visit a doctor to make sure you do not have more serious conditions such as colon cancer, inflammatory bowel disease, or

---

[2] Meyer, D, and M Stasse-Wolthuis. "The Bifidogenic Effect of Inulin and Oligofructose and Its Consequences for Gut Health." European Journal of Clinical Nutrition, vol. 63, no. 11, 2009, pp. 1277–1289., doi:10.1038/ejcn.2009.64.

celiac disease.[3] Your doctor will be asking you a series of questions that will help them determine if you are suffering from IBS, which are the following:

1. Have you had recurring stomach pain at least one day a week?

2. Have you had a change in the number of stools? They will also ask you about the appearance of your stools.

3. Have you had these issues for at least three months?

If you have answered "yes" to all these questions, it would be wise to speak to your doctor about the possibility of you having IBS. Approximately 14% of United States citizens have IBS, which is expected to rise; in fact, most with IBS have probably gone undiagnosed.[4] Currently, 20% of people within the United Kingdom and about 10-15% of people in the United States[5] suffer from IBS.

There also exist many continued studies that suggest positive results from following a low FODMAP diet, specifically for those who are suffering from inflammatory bowel diseases (IBD), like ulcerative colitis and Crohn's disease.[6]

---

[3] "Diagnosis and Management of Irritable Bowel Syndrome in Adults in Primary Care: Summary of NICE Guidance." Bmj, vol. 350, no. Mar 03 16, Mar. 2015, doi:10.1136/bmj.h1216.

[4] Hungin, A. P. S., et al. "Irritable Bowel Syndrome in the United States: Prevalence, Symptom Patterns and Impact." Alimentary Pharmacology and Therapeutics, vol. 21, no. 11, 2005, pp. 1365–1375., doi:10.1111/j.1365-2036.2005.02463.x.

[5] "Irritable Bowel Syndrome." American College of Gastrinology. https://gi.org/topics/irritable-bowel-syndrome/.

[6] Gearry, Richard B., et al. "Reduction of Dietary Poorly Absorbed Short-Chain Carbohydrates (FODMAPs) Improves Abdominal Symptoms in Patients with Inflammatory Bowel Disease — A Pilot Study." Journal of Crohns and Colitis, vol. 3, no. 1, 2009, pp. 8–14., doi:10.1016/j.crohns.2008.09.004.

You should consider starting the low FODMAP diet if you have not responded to stress management or have ongoing gut issues. There is also further research being conducted for those suffering from exercise-induced digestive complications, as well as diverticulitis.[7] Consult with your doctor to determine if a low FODMAP diet would be a good choice for you.

It is also important to note that if you have a current or prior history with an eating disorder, or if you are underweight, you should not consider following a low FODMAP diet. Because this is a restrictive diet, it may place more restrictions on current foods you eat, which is not a lifestyle that will benefit you. It is also recommended to speak with your dietitian and medical doctor if you are pregnant before committing to this type of diet.

Benefits of a Low FODMAP Diet

There have been extensive studies into how people who suffer from IBS can show improvement in their symptoms through using a low FODMAP diet.[8] Some main benefits that can be experienced include the following:

- Reduction in symptoms of digestive issues

- Positively impacted quality of life

- Improved mental health

- Noticing quick results

---

[7] Lis, Dana, et al. "Case Study: Utilizing a Low FODMAP Diet to Combat Exercise-Induced Gastrointestinal Symptoms." International Journal of Sport Nutrition and Exercise Metabolism, vol. 26, no. 5, 2016, pp. 481–487., doi:10.1123/ijsnem.2015-0293.

[8] Marsh, Abigail, et al. "Does a Diet Low in FODMAPs Reduce Symptoms Associated with Functional Gastrointestinal Disorders? A Comprehensive Systematic Review and Meta-Analysis." European Journal of Nutrition, vol. 55, no. 3, 2015, pp. 897–906., doi:10.1007/s00394-015-0922-1.

Reduction in Symptoms of Digestive Issues

The symptoms of IBS specifically have a wide variety; however, the main symptoms that you can experience are bowel urgency, flatulence, reflux, bloating, and stomach pain. In fact, out of these main symptoms, stomach pain is found to be a problem for more than 80% of those who suffer with IBS.[9] When these symptoms become a common occurrence, they can even become crippling when trying to plan your day around them.

The good news is that you will no longer need to focus your day on your symptoms with the low FODMAP diet, as the main symptoms of bloating and stomach pain are significantly diminished. In fact, some medical studies have shown a 75% to 81% decrease in bloating and stomach pains in patients on a low FODMAP diet.[10] Management of other symptoms such as constipation, diarrhea, and flatulence have also shown improvements through varying scientific studies.[11]

Positively Impacted Quality of Life

Another common theme reported with sufferers of IBS is that their quality of life is impacted negatively. However, several medical studies have shown that these individuals can improve this

---

[9] Drossman, Douglas A., and William L. Hasler. "Rome IV—Functional GI Disorders: Disorders of Gut-Brain Interaction." Gastroenterology, vol. 150, no. 6, 2016, pp. 1257–1261., doi:10.1053/j.gastro.2016.03.035.

[10] Marsh, Abigail, et al. "Does a Diet Low in FODMAPs Reduce Symptoms Associated with Functional Gastrointestinal Disorders? A Comprehensive Systematic Review and Meta-Analysis." European Journal of Nutrition, vol. 55, no. 3, 2015, pp. 897–906., doi:10.1007/s00394-015-0922-1.

[11] Böhn, Lena, et al. "Diet Low in FODMAPs Reduces Symptoms of Irritable Bowel Syndrome as Well as Traditional Dietary Advice: A Randomized Controlled Trial." Gastroenterology, vol. 149, no. 6, 2015, doi:10.1053/j.gastro.2015.07.054.

hardship significantly when they follow a low FODMAP diet.[12] Scientists believe that the main factor is that energy levels of those with IBS is increased, and these researchers plan to follow up with more medical studies to confirm with placebo-controlled evidence.[13]

Improved Mental Health

For those who have been suffering from the effects of digestive orders for a considerable amount of time, it probably doesn't just affect their physical health, but their mental health as well. In fact, many chronic sufferers report they have common problems with depression and anxiety. When you diminish or eliminate symptoms associated with digestive disorders, your mental health will also be improved, as you will be lowering your stress levels that comes along with these disorders.[14]

Noticing Quick Results

Many who try a low FODMAP diet will start to see positive results in six weeks or less, while others may even see much improvement in less than two weeks after limiting and eliminating high FODMAPS from their diets. Since there is a high probability that you will see these results quickly, it is worth giving it a chance to improve your life in a short period. At the very least, you are improving your overall health by reducing and eliminating particularly unhealthy foods from your digestive tract.

---

[12] Marsh, Abigail, et al. "Does a Diet Low in FODMAPs Reduce Symptoms Associated with Functional Gastrointestinal Disorders? A Comprehensive Systematic Review and Meta-Analysis." European Journal of Nutrition, vol. 55, no. 3, 2015, pp. 897–906., doi:10.1007/s00394-015-0922-1.

[13] Staudacher, Heidi M., et al. "Fermentable Carbohydrate Restriction Reduces Luminal Bifidobacteria and Gastrointestinal Symptoms in Patients with Irritable Bowel Syndrome." The Journal of Nutrition, vol. 142, no. 8, 2012, pp. 1510–1518., doi:10.3945/jn.112.159285.

[14] Lydiard, R. Bruce. "Gastrointestinal Disorders, Irritable Bowel Syndrome, and Anxiety." Anxiety Disorders, 2015, pp. 255–266., doi:10.1093/med/9780199395125.003.0018.

What Are the Drawbacks?

Due to the low FODMAP diet's restrictive nature, it is recommended that you have guidance from a medical doctor or nutritionist while following it.

It can be somewhat of a challenge to eat out at restaurants, especially during the first two phases. However, there are several tips mentioned in chapter 14 that will help you overcome this obstacle.

It can be especially challenging for those that eat a vegetarian diet due to their having to remove legumes and various fruits and vegetables from their diets. However, there are supplements that you can take to ensure you are receiving the correct amount of nutrients, while still having a wide range of fruits and vegetables that you can enjoy.

Chapter Summary

- FODMAP foods are carbohydrates that are resistant to digestion. Typically, these are classified as dietary fiber; however, those with sensitive digestive tracts will have particular issues, resulting in gut disorders and discomforts.

- Those diagnosed with IBS will see the greatest benefit from following this diet, and those who suffer from typical digestive tract imbalance symptoms will see a reduction in stomach pains, bloating, gas, and diarrhea.

- One benefit that you can experience is a heightened quality of life after reducing your chronic symptoms. Those whose lives revolve around their symptoms will find relief and will be able to free themselves from having to center their lives around their disorder.

In the next chapter, you will learn about the process of a low FODMAP diet through three phases you will need to implement.

Chapter Two:
How to Start on a Low FODMAP Diet

Before starting this process, it is crucial that you consult with your healthcare provider or a medical doctor first. They will run some tests and ask you questions to rule out other medical issues that may be causing your IBS and gastrointestinal issues, which is an important step because other chronic conditions can also be the cause; if you cannot identify the cause, you cannot determine whether a low FODMAP diet will help you or make your symptoms worse. When these conditions go unchecked, they can cause long-term damage to your body, so for the sake of your overall health, it is wise to seek your medical doctor's advice and expertise beforehand.

There are three steps that you need to follow to start a low FODMAP diet properly, and it is wise to speak to a registered dietitian prior to starting, as they will be the ones to help guide you if you should encounter any obstacles. They can also give you some guidance in terms of other foods that could be affecting you personally.

A common misconception with the food in this diet is that it is flavorless because you need to eliminate onions and garlic; however, you will find that there is a wide range of spices, such as turmeric, saffron, black pepper, mustard seeds, lemongrass, ginger, fenugreek, and chives, which are all low in FODMAPs, that will help flavor your dishes, specifically those in the recipe section of this book.

With this diet, you will be able to use garlic-infused oil, which requires garlic to be strained. Even though garlic is used in making this oil, garlic is not fat soluble, which means the flavor is simply transferred to the oil rather than the garlic itself. As a result, this type of oil will give you flavoring without the FODMAP symptoms that are related to garlic.

Phase 1 — The Elimination Period

After speaking to your dietitian, set a date for when you plan to remove all high-level FODMAPS from your diet. Refer to the list in chapter 1 and ensure that you have eliminated all the foods listed. It is highly recommended that you completely eliminate all the high FODMAP foods during the first phase because, if you do not, there is a chance that this diet will not work for you. This diet does not work if you are not eliminating personally triggering foods.

If you find there are staples that you cannot quite give up, talk to your dietitian to learn about substitutes that can work for you on this diet. This phase will last 2 to 4 weeks. It is ideal to wait until you are not experiencing symptoms of digestive problems, so that the next phase will become more effective. The good news is that, if foods high in FODMAPs are causing your gut symptoms, you will likely experience relief from your symptoms in a few days once you start the first phase.

This is one aspect of this diet, and it is important. You need to do your best to eliminate all foods on the list; remind yourself that it will be for a short period. The purpose of taking these foods out of your diet is to determine which foods are giving your digestive system problems and resulting in your symptoms. Eliminating these foods will give your body an opportunity to flush these foods out of your system, helping to reset itself.

Be gentle with yourself during this period because there will be times that you are going to be tempted to eat foods restricted by the list while at work or out with friends. Keep your mind on your personal goals and your overall health—this short period will help improve your overall well-being, as well as your quality of life.

Even if you slip up and eat a high FODMAP food, do not fret; although, it would be helpful for you to keep a journal of your experiences, as doing so will help you to better understand how different foods affect your body. In case you eat a high FODMAP food during this phase, your journaling your symptoms will help you determine early if you will need to eliminate it from your diet altogether. This leads us into the next phase.

Phase 2 — Reintroduction of High FODMAP Foods

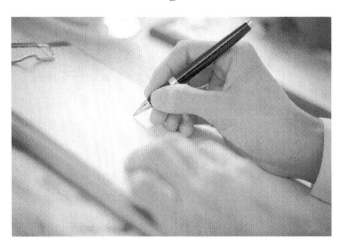

The purpose of this next phase is to determine which high FODMAP foods are triggering your symptoms and the level at which you can tolerate them. During this phase, make a list of any high FODMAP foods you regularly ate before starting this diet. Then, break it down on a calendar. You will want to consume a small portion of each food for three days, then you will need to pay attention to signs your body gives and record how each FODMAP affected you.

Some foods will have a larger impact on your health than others. This, in particular, needs to be monitored, as you may simply need to restrict or diminish the amount of a particular food you are consuming if you are only feeling slightly agitated by any symptoms after a three-day trial period.[15] In terms of the FODMAPs that bring back your symptoms in full force, they will probably need to be permanently eliminated from your diet, if possible.

---

[15] Gibson, Peter R, and Susan J Shepherd. "Evidence-Based Dietary Management of Functional Gastrointestinal Symptoms: The FODMAP Approach." Journal of Gastroenterology and Hepatology, vol. 25, no. 2, 2010, pp. 252–258., doi:10.1111/j.1440-1746.2009.06149.x.

As an example, say that you loved eating foods with apples before—eat a full apple and determine if your symptoms are returning. You will want to do this for each food on the list to see which ones were most likely a cause for your digestive issues. Remember to go through the entire list of previously eaten high FODMAPs because you may have more than one type of food that is triggering your digestive symptoms. This list will be quite extensive, so this phase will last anywhere from 6 to 8 weeks.

As an important note, while going through this stage, you need to maintain a low FODMAP diet other than the high FODMAP food you are testing. Even if you find that you can tolerate a particular high FODMAP food, it needs to continue to be restricted until phase 3. Also, know that sensitivities to certain FODMAPs are different from food allergies, as they are just causing upsets to your digestive system—not resulting in common allergy symptoms such as hives or rashes.

Phase 3 — Personalization of Your Future Eating Habits

This phase is where you will continue to monitor which foods are bringing back any symptoms. During this stage, you will create your personalized diet for the long term that will improve your intestinal health and quality of life.[16] You may find that any foods that bothered you during phase 2 can be eaten in smaller amounts or less frequently. If you find that you continue to eat a bothersome food item in any amount, it may need to be eliminated altogether. This phase is arguably the longest if you have a complicated list of foods you cannot tolerate, and finding the correct balance of consumption and frequency may take some time.

It is important to remember that there will be times when you will accidentally eat these foods, and this is not a time to become upset with yourself. You are learning the mechanics of your body and how it reacts, and it will always be a learning process. You may find that foods that you were once able to tolerate start to trigger your symptoms, and it can also

---

[16] Meyer, D, and M Stasse-Wolthuis. "The Bifidogenic Effect of Inulin and Oligofructose and Its Consequences for Gut Health." European Journal of Clinical Nutrition, vol. 63, no. 11, 2009, pp. 1277–1289., doi:10.1038/ejcn.2009.64.

be a combination of foods not conducive to your overall gut health. Remember that stress can have a large impact on your intestinal health, so continue to be kind and gentle with yourself as you go through this process.

Chapter Summary

- The first phase is where you will eliminate high FODMAP foods from your diet. It will last anywhere from 2 to 4 weeks and allows your body to eliminate these foods and symptoms associated with them.

- Phase 2 is a lengthy process that can take up to two months. You will start to slowly and individually reintroduce high FODMAP foods into your diet to determine which of them cause you digestive upset symptoms.

- As you continue to learn how your body reacts to certain types of foods, phase 3 will help you monitor your body's changes as you continue to lessen or eliminate your digestive symptoms.

In the next chapter, you will learn more about acceptable foods you should put on your grocery list, how to save money while shopping, and also about a week-long meal plan to follow.

Chapter Three:
Seven Day Meal Plan

Sometimes, it will be difficult to know where to begin. However, using this introductory guide for your first week with a low FODMAP diet will help you. These are recipes found within this cookbook, so it will make it even more simple to get started today. You may find it helpful to plan out your weekly meals either on your computer or on your personal electronic device.

7 Day Sample Menu for a Low FODMAP Diet

Day 1

Breakfast — Oatmeal with strawberries and walnuts

Lunch — Grilled chicken salad, cucumbers, and feta cheese

Snack — fruit smoothie

Dinner — Flat iron steak with roasted zucchini

Dessert — Peanut butter cookie

Day 2

Breakfast — Oatmeal with blueberries

Lunch — Shrimp zoodles with roasted carrots

Snack — Roasted almonds

Dinner — Maple mustard chicken with pineapple chunks

Dessert — Rice pudding

Day 3

Breakfast — Scrambled tofu and coffee

Lunch — Bacon chicken wrap with sweet potato fries

Snack — Walnuts

Dinner — Cod fillet and brown rice

Dessert — Sliced pineapple

Day 4

Breakfast — Overnight peanut butter with banana oats and pecans

Lunch — Baked lemon pepper chicken

Snack — Carrot sticks and peanut butter

Dinner — Creamy beef strips and Cobb salad

Dessert — Vanilla cinnamon bites

Day 5

Breakfast — French toast and strawberries

Lunch — Turkey burger patties

Snack — Oat bar

Dinner — Beef stir fry

Dessert — Key lime cheesecake

Day 6

Breakfast — Sweet potato toast with mashed avocado

Lunch — Cod bites and quinoa salad

Snack — Mint mocha bite

Dinner — Ham mac and cheese casserole

Dessert — Sliced strawberries

Day 7

Breakfast — Almond butter smoothie

Lunch — Quinoa salad with chicken, zucchini, and radishes

Snack — Popcorn

Dinner — Lamb chops with glazed edamame

Dessert — Chocolate mousse

The Importance of Shopping Lists

To help you to stay on track, be sure to create a shopping list instead of aimlessly looking for foods that are low in FODMAPs. Not only will this extra preparation save you time, but it will also help you to save money because you will be more prone to sticking to your list. The easiest way to create your list is to determine which meals you plan to make in between your trips to the grocery store and buy only what you require.

Look in your refrigerator, freezer, and pantry, and be sure to use foods that you already have on hand. Doing so will also help you to keep your food budget to a minimum, as you will be eating foods that you have already purchased. You might even find that you have enough food to make some meals without going to the grocery store as often.

When you visit the grocery store, be sure to stay away from isles that have items specifically high in FODMAPs. Doing so will help remove the temptation to buy these foods while you are in the elimination step, and it will also help you from buying off of your shopping list. As a general rule, do *not* shop when you are hungry—

if you do, you will probably find an excuse to buy more than what is on your list because you will want to satisfy your hunger. Instead, go shopping after a meal or eat a quick snack before leaving.

Simple Shopping List Guide

Even though there are over 100 recipes included in the recipe section of this book, you can use this section as a handy guide to help you purchase foods that are low in FODMAPs, so you can create your own meals.

Vegetables — There are a variety of vegetables that you can enjoy and eat raw, sautéed, roasted, or baked. You can also get creative with different flavors by using spices. Vegetables are a great addition to your main meals or even as an easy snack to bring to work. Low FODMAP vegetables include:

zucchini, spinach, kale, carrots, squash, sweet potatoes, eggplant, Bok choy, olives, lettuce, celery, cucumber, radish, turnips, and bean sprouts

It is important to note that you need to keep sweet potatoes to one-half cup or less per serving, as it can become a high FODMAP food when eaten in excess.

Fruits — Incorporating fruits into your meals is easy, and it helps to add variety to your plate. You can use fruits as a snack, a topping for your foods, or even as a dessert. Low FODMAP fruits include:

strawberries, rhubarb, pineapple, papaya, oranges, lemons, mandarins, limes, kiwi, blueberries, bananas, grapes, and cantaloupe

Protein — Being an important macronutrient, protein is essential to a balanced diet, especially if you are eating vegan or vegetarian meals. Proteins do not always need to come from meat products, though it needs to comprise 35% of your daily calories. Proteins low in FODMAPs include:

firm tofu, prawns, pork, lamb, fish, chicken, and beef

Whole grains — Since you are unable to eat wheat products with a low FODMAP diet, you will need to find other sources of grains that will be gentler on your gut and easily digestible. Incorporating whole grains into your balanced diet will also help your digestive system work at optimal levels, allowing you to continue to see your health improve. Examples include:

quinoa, gluten-free oats, millet, maize, buckwheat, sorghum, tapioca, brown rice, and sourdough bread

Dairy — This can be a tricky category, as many dairy products contain lactose. Be sure to read the labels on any products that you buy, as additives are often included. Low FODMAP dairy items include:

Parmesan cheese, cheddar cheese, brie, Camembert, feta cheese, other soft cheeses, almond milk, coconut milk, and lactose-free milk

Nuts — These are a superfood that will give you various vitamins and minerals. They are a source high in protein, fats, and fiber, and having a serving of nuts every day will help you balance out your gut and continue to better your overall health. Be sure to consume unsalted and raw nuts to benefit your health the most. Examples of low FODMAP nuts include:

walnuts, pine nuts, pecans, peanuts, macadamia nuts, and almonds

Seeds — Like nuts, seeds can provide many types of vitamins and minerals essential to your gut and overall health. To reap the greatest benefit, they also need to be raw and unroasted without salt. Low FODMAP seed examples are:

sunflower, sesame, pumpkin, and linseeds

Beverages — Drinks you consume are important to helping your body reach optimal health. Drinking fluids with high sugar counts are the most likely to impact your digestive and overall health, and they can also lead to more serious issues. You will need to ensure that you are hydrated too, so your body can function properly. Drinks that you are able to have on a low FODMAP diet are the following:

water, white tea, peppermint tea, green tea, coffee, and black tea

Snacks — Your snack list is endless, as you are able to have a variety of fruits, vegetables, nuts, and seeds as a snack as well. Snacks are important in helping keep your energy levels up during long periods between meals. They will also help keep your brain working at its full potential, as well as your digestive system. Other examples of snacks include:

popcorn, brown rice cakes, and dark chocolate

Sweeteners — There are a variety of sweeteners that you can add to your foods that are also low in FODMAPs. It is wise to keep these to a minimum in your drinks and meals, but just a bit once in a while goes far with your available choices, which include:

maple syrup, brown sugar, Stevia, and molasses

Oils — These cannot only be used to sauté and brown your food, but they can be a great additive of flavor. Low FODMAP oils include:

extra virgin olive oil, coconut oil, garlic infused olive oil, almond butter, and coconut butter

Condiments — These are great additions to foods and can add a great variety to your meals. Common low FODMAP condiments include the following:

wasabi powder, white rice vinegar, salt, black pepper, mustard, pesto, ginger, and basil

You will find a wide variety of sauces and condiments that you can use to add some variety to your meals in chapter 13

It is important to note that reading ingredients lists on any packaged items for restricted FODMAPs is a *must*. You should look for items such as fructose or low-sugar sweeteners especially, as they are additives for foods that you would not necessarily suspect. FODMAPs are generally added to foods as a substitute for sugar, fat, or as a source of prebiotics.

Ways to Save Money

If you can buy items in bulk, it will end up saving you more money in the long run, and these items can also be used for other areas of your life. It is important to look for sale items or even online shopping networks to help you to keep in budget. Remember to look at labels and be sure to get gluten-free and unsweetened products when you can, as FODMAPs can be an additive in unexpected, pre-packaged foods. Be sure to shop around for the best prices and educate yourself on item prices, so you know you are getting the best deal; however, you should also be aware that quality may vary depending on brand and price.

Once you have an idea from what you already have stocked in your kitchen, make sure you try to use those items first and not buy more, unless it is an item you will use regularly. When you throw food out, it is equivalent to throwing money out with it.

One way to cut down costs is to make almond flour and coconut flour in your own kitchen. Almond flour can be created by using a high-powered blender and pulsing raw, unsalted almonds. Doing so will also ensure the freshness of your final product. You would also follow the same process with meat of coconut once it has been dried, saving you from needing to buy a more expensive product at the grocery store. You will gain a sense of accomplishment and confidence when you're making your own flour.

Buying ingredient components in bulk will also cut down on costs. For example, instead of buying cheese already shredded, compare the prices to buying a block of the same cheese and grating it yourself. The time it takes to accomplish this is minimal, and you will feel a difference in your pocket. It also helps when recipes call for the same type of cheese and it needs to be grated versus shredded.

Another tip is to look for sale prices and use weekly coupons in the Sunday paper or deals offered by grocery stores. Most items can be packed and stored in your freezer for later. This is especially true for fruits and vegetables, as they are cheaper when they are in season. It also gives you an opportunity to enjoy these foods off season.

Looking for meats, fruits, vegetables, and cheeses at your local farmers market is a great tip, as they are the mom and pop growers that rely on you to keep them in business. They will also have organic and GMO-free options, so shop local whenever possible. If you do, you will feel better all around, inside and out, for helping your local community grow themselves.

Alternatively, you can look on Amazon.com and have your ingredients delivered straight to your doorstep without the hassle. You will find that ingredient prices for items you use most will probably be cheaper, even with shipping. However, remember that you need to make sure you carefully observe the ingredients list for additives that are high in FODMAPs while on Amazon.

This next tip is actually both a time and money saver: you can double any of these recipes or even save leftovers for eating later. Doing so will make sure you do not have to cook for every snack or meal, and you will have time to make other dishes if you prefer.

Nutritional Information Note for This Cookbook

Nutritional information for the recipes provided in the next few chapters is an *approximate only*. Any substitutions that you use will alter nutritional values and need to be personally researched. As such, I cannot guarantee complete accuracy of any nutritional information given for recipes in this cookbook.

Chapter Summary

- Pay special attention to serving amounts of sweet potatoes, pumpkin puree, and avocados, so you do not consume high amounts of FODMAPS that may slow down your progress.

- Being aware of sales and buying in bulk will save you time and money at the grocery store. Freeze and store fruits and vegetables in season, so you can enjoy them year-round.

- Creating a shopping list will help you to stay under your budget, as well as keep you focused on what you really need at the grocery store. Be sure to take an inventory of any food items you have on hand, so you are not buying additional items that you have stored in your freezer, fridge, and pantry.

In the next chapter, we will be taking a look at some low FODMAP recipes for your use.

Chapter Four:
Breakfast and Smoothie Recipes

Almond Butter Smoothie

Total Prep and Cooking Time: 5 minutes

Makes: 2 Smoothies

Protein: 14g

Carbohydrates: 24g

Fat: 24g

Sodium: 196g

Fiber: 2g

Calories: 344

What you need:

- 3 cups almond milk, unsweetened

- 12 ice cubes

- ¼ tsp. pure almond extract, sugar-free

- 1 tbsp. ground cinnamon

- ¼ cup flax meal

- 30 drops Stevia sweetener, liquid

- ¼ cup almond butter, unsalted and softened

40

Steps:

1. Combine almond milk, ground cinnamon, flax meal, almond extract, liquid Stevia, ice cubes, and almond butter into a blender.

2. Pulse for 60 seconds or until consistency is smooth.

3. Divide into two serving cups and enjoy!

Banana Smoothie

Total Prep and Cooking Time: 5 minutes

Makes: 2 Smoothies

Protein: 15g

Carbohydrates: 53g

Fat: 5g

Sodium: 81g

Fiber: 7g

Calories: 274

What you need:

- 2 medium bananas, peeled and sliced

- ¼ tsp. ground nutmeg

- 1 cup almond milk, unsweetened

- ½ cup gluten-free rolled oats

- 1 tsp. pure vanilla extract, sugar-free

- ¼ tsp. ground cinnamon

- 1 tsp. pure maple syrup

- ¼ cup canned coconut milk, chilled

Steps:

1. Open a can of coconut milk and empty out the liquid in a lidded container to use in a different recipe.

2. Use a food blender to pulse maple syrup, nutmeg, cinnamon, vanilla extract, solid coconut milk, oats, almond milk, and bananas for approximately 60 seconds or until it is a smooth consistency.

3. Divide between 2 glasses and enjoy immediately!

Berry Smoothie

Total Prep and Cooking Time:
5 minutes

Makes: 2 Smoothies

Protein: 10g

Carbohydrates: 55g

Fat: 6g

Sodium: 117g

Fiber: 6g

Calories: 293

What you need:

- 1 cup blueberries, frozen
- 2 cups almond milk, unsweetened
- 2 medium bananas
- ⅛ tsp. ground cinnamon
- 1 cup strawberries, frozen

Steps:

1. Pulse blueberries, almond milk, bananas, and strawberries in a food blender for approximately 60 seconds or until a smooth consistency.

2. Distribute to 2 glasses and dust with cinnamon. Enjoy immediately!

Blueberry Pancakes

Total Prep and Cooking Time:
15 minutes

Makes: 4 Pancakes

Protein: 2g

Carbohydrates: 24g

Fat: 10g

Sodium: 108g

Fiber: 3g

Calories: 189

What you need:

- ⅓ cup almond milk, unsweetened

- ½ cup pancake mix, gluten-free

- 1 medium banana, mashed

- ⅛ cup gelatin collagen powder, separated

- ⅔ tsp. pure vanilla extract, sugar-free

- 1 tsp. coconut oil, melted

- 1 cup blueberries

- 4 tsp. coconut oil, separated

- 1⅓ tbsp. pure maple syrup

Steps:

1. Empty 1 teaspoon of coconut oil in a mug and nuke for 30 seconds or until liquefied.

2. In the meantime, use a medium dish to mash the banana with a spoon or potato masher.

3. Blend melted coconut oil, vanilla extract, pancake mix, and almond milk with the banana until a smooth consistency.

4. Combine gelatin collagen power and blend until smooth. Add 1 to 2 teaspoons of additional almond milk if too thick.

5. Fold in blueberries carefully into the batter.

6. Warm a small skillet over medium heat and empty 1 teaspoon of coconut oil.

7. Allow the coconut oil to dissolve and move the pan so it is coated completely.

8. Ladle ¼ of batter into the base of the pan and heat for 2 minutes before flipping.

9. Heat for an additional 60 seconds and transfer to a serving plate.

10. Repeat steps 6 through 9 for the other 3 pancakes.

11. Top each with maple syrup and enjoy while warm.

Breakfast Wrap

Total Prep and Cooking Time: 5 minutes

Makes: 4 Helpings

Protein: 9g

Carbohydrates: 15g

Fat: 13g

Sodium: 156g

Fiber: 3g

Calories: 205

What you need:

- 4 corn tortillas
- 8 slices cheddar cheese
- 2 cups spinach leaves
- ½ cup avocado

Steps:

1. Remove the shell from an avocado and mash in a glass dish.

2. Rinse spinach leaves and shake to remove excess water.

3. Arrange tortillas on a flat surface.

4. Evenly divide and layer avocado, spinach leaves, and cheddar cheese on each.

5. Rotate to enclose, starting at the base.

6. Enjoy immediately.

Cinnamon Almond Crepes

Total Prep and Cooking Time:
20 minutes

Makes: 4 Crepes

Protein: 3g

Carbohydrates: 17g

Fat: 11g

Sodium: 29g

Fiber: 2g

Calories: 165

What you need:

- ½ cup almond flour*

- 2 medium bananas

- ¼ tsp. pure vanilla extract, sugar-free

- 1 cup almond milk, separated

- ¼ tsp. ground cinnamon

- 2.67 tbsp. extra virgin olive oil, separated

49

Steps:

1. Empty 2 teaspoons of olive oil into a skillet and allow it to warm up.

2. In the meantime, blend almond milk, bananas, vanilla extract, cinnamon, and almond flour in a glass dish with an electric beater for 45 seconds.

3. Transfer a ladle of batter to the pan and swirl it around to distribute it evenly around.

4. Heat for 30 seconds or until edges turn darker, then turn to the other side.

5. Warm for an additional 30 seconds, then transfer to a serving platter. Enclose with tin foil.

6. Empty another 2 teaspoons in the skillet and repeat steps 3 through 6 until you have completed 8 crepes.

7. Enjoy immediately with your favorite fruits or compote.

* You can also substitute homemade gluten-free flour with the recipe found in chapter 13.

Cranberry Orange Smoothie

Total Prep and Cooking Time: 5 minutes

Makes: 2 Smoothies

Protein: 3g

Carbohydrates: 38g

Fat: 1g

Sodium: 18g

Fiber: 4g

Calories: 164

What you need:

- 1⅛ cups orange juice, freshly squeezed

- 1 cup cranberries, raw

- ¼ cup almond milk, unsweetened

- 1 medium banana

- 1 tbsp. lemon juice

- 1 tsp. pure maple syrup

- 1 cup ice cubes

Steps:

1. Use a glass dish to squeeze orange juice and remove the seeds.

2. Transfer to a food blender and pulse cranberries, almond milk, banana, lemon juice, maple syrup, and ice until it reaches your desired consistency.

3. Divide between two glasses and enjoy immediately!

French Toast

Total Prep and Cooking Time: 25 minutes

Makes: 4 Helpings

Protein: 11g

Carbohydrates: 26g

Fat: 10g

Sodium: 184g

Fiber: 1g

Calories: 230

What you need:

- 1 cup almond milk, unsweetened

- 1⅓ cup tofu, firm and plain

- 2 tsp. pure vanilla extract, sugar-free

- 4 slices gluten-free bread of your choice

- 4 tsp. extra virgin olive oil, separated

- 2 tbsp. pure maple syrup

Steps:

1. Use a food blender to pulse vanilla extract, almond milk, and tofu until a smooth consistency.

2. Add 2 teaspoons of olive oil into a large skillet and warm.

3. Transfer the wet mix to a shallow dish and immerse the bread in it for 60 seconds on each side. Transfer to a plate until ready to brown.

4. Cook 2 slices at once for 3 minutes on each side, then transfer to a serving platter.

5. Repeat for remaining slices of bread until complete.

6. Top with maple syrup and enjoy while warm.

Green Hibiscus Smoothie

Total Prep and Cooking Time: 10 minutes

Makes: 2 Smoothies

Protein: 2g

Carbohydrates: 8g

Fat: 12g

Sodium: 11g

Fiber: 3g

Calories: 142

What you need:

- 1 hibiscus tea bag
- ½ inch ginger root, peeled
- ½ cup water
- 1 cup zucchini, cubed
- ½ cup raspberries, frozen
- ½ cup coconut milk, liquid

Steps:

1. Empty water into a mug and nuke in the microwave for 1 minute.

2. Insert the tea bag and allow it to steep for 5 minutes.

3. In the meantime, scrub zucchini and chop into small cubes. Transfer to a food blender.

4. Wash raspberries and shake to remove excess water. Transfer to the food blender.

5. Remove the tea bag from the water, and empty into the blender.

6. Combine ginger and coconut milk in the blender and pulse for approximately 30 seconds or until smooth.

7. Transfer to two glasses and enjoy immediately!

Hearty Oatmeal

Total Prep and Cooking Time: 10 minutes

Makes: 4 Helpings

Protein: 8g

Carbohydrates: 45g

Fat: 3g

Sodium: 300g

Fiber: 8g

Calories: 171

What you need:

- 4 cups water
- ½ tsp. iodized salt
- 2 cups gluten-free rolled oats
- ½ tsp. ground cloves
- 1 tsp. ground cinnamon
- 4 tbsp. chia seeds
- ½ tsp. ground nutmeg
- 4 tbsp. pure maple syrup

Steps:

1. Empty salt and water into a saucepan and warm on the highest heat setting until it starts to bubble.

2. Combine oats into hot water and heat for 5 minutes while occasionally tossing.

3. Blend ground cloves, chia seeds, ground cinnamon, ground nutmeg, and maple syrup, then warm for another 5 minutes.

4. Serve immediately and enjoy!

Immune Boosting Smoothie

Total Prep and Cooking Time:
10 minutes

Makes: 2 Smoothies

Protein: 3g

Carbohydrates: 9g

Fat: 1g

Sodium: 221g

What you need:

- 2 cups spinach

- 1-inch ginger root, peeled

- 2 kale leaves

- 2 medium rib celery

- ⅛ tsp. iodized salt

- 2 medium cucumber

Fiber: 3g

- 2 tbsp. lime juice

Calories: 49

- 2 cups ice

Steps:

1. Thoroughly rinse spinach, celery, and kale, then shake to remove any extra water. Remove the tough ends of the kale and discard.

2. Scrub cucumbers well and chop into small sections.

3. Use a food blender to pulse salt, lime juice, ginger, cucumbers, celery, kale, and spinach until a smooth consistency.

4. Combine ice and continue to pulse until it reaches your desired consistency.

5. Distribute to two glasses and enjoy immediately!

Peanut Butter and Banana Overnight Oats

Total Prep and Cooking Time:
5 minutes + overnight

Makes: 4 Helpings

Protein: 19g

Carbohydrates: 60g

Fat: 14g

Sodium: 158g

Fiber: 13g

Calories: 359

What you need:

- 2 cups gluten-free rolled oats

- 4 tsp. chia seeds

- 2 medium bananas, mashed

- 4 tbsp. peanut butter, natural and no sugar added

- 2 cups almond milk, unsweetened

- 1 tsp. ground cinnamon

Steps:

1. Blend cinnamon, almond milk, peanut butter, bananas, chia seeds, and oats in a glass dish.

2. Toss to combine fully and cover with a layer of plastic wrap.

3. Transfer to the refrigerator and serve the next morning immediately if you desire it cold. If you prefer hot, nuke in the microwave for 60 seconds before enjoying.

Quinoa Tofu Scramble

Total Prep and Cooking Time: 20 minutes

Makes: 4 Helpings

Protein: 9g

Carbohydrates: 3g

Fat: 8g

Sodium: 311g

Fiber: 2g

Calories: 117

What you need:

- ½ tsp. iodized salt, separated

- 3 tsp. garlic infused olive oil*

- 8 oz. pre-pressed tofu, firm

- ½ tsp. turmeric powder

- 2 cups spinach

- ¼ tsp. black pepper

Steps:

1. Ensure the quinoa is properly rinsed under cold water. Transfer to a deep pot and blend ¼ teaspoon of salt with water.

2. Heat on the highest setting until the fluid is starting to bubble, then turn the burner temperature down. Warm for an

additional 12 minutes or until fluid is fully reduced.

3. In the meantime, set out a skillet and empty garlic-infused olive oil to start warming.

4. Rinse spinach well and shake to remove excess moisture. Set aside.

5. Break tofu into small sections and put it into the pan. Combine the leftover ¼ teaspoon of salt, turmeric, and black pepper until fully incorporated.

6. Warm the mixture on the stove for approximately 3 minutes while continuously tossing.

7. Toss in spinach and continue to stir continuously for an additional 2 minutes.

8. Layer quinoa and tofu scramble into each serving dish.

9. Serve immediately and enjoy!

  * *You can make your own homemade version with the recipe found in chapter 13.*

Scrambled Tofu

Total Prep and Cooking Time: 10 minutes

Makes: 4 Helpings

Protein: 19g

Carbohydrates: 11g

Fat: 13g

Sodium: 137g

Fiber: 4g

Calories: 224

What you need:

- 1 lb. pre-pressed tofu, firm
- 1 cup water
- 4 tsp. gluten-free soy sauce*
- 1 tsp. ground turmeric
- 2 cup carrots, chopped finely
- 1 tbsp. garlic infused olive oil**

Steps:

1. Use a glass dish to blend turmeric, soy sauce, and water until integrated.

2. Scrub carrots and chop into small sections. Transfer to the dish.

3. Break apart tofu into smaller sections into the dish, then toss to combine fully.

4. Empty garlic-infused olive oil into a skillet and warm over the medium setting of heat.

5. Distribute the mixture into the pan and toss occasionally while it heats for 5 minutes.

6. Remove with a slotted spoon and serve immediately. Enjoy!

If you are unable to find gluten-free soy sauce, tamari is a great gluten-free substitute.

**You can make your own, homemade version of olive oil with the recipe found in chapter 13.*

Sweet Potato Toast

Total Prep and Cooking Time: 25 minutes

Makes: 4 Helpings

Protein: 2g

Carbohydrates: 25g

Fat: 0g

Sodium: 34g

Fiber: 3g

Calories: 107

What you need:

- 2 large sweet potatoes

- 2 tbsp. pure maple syrup

Steps:

1. Set your oven to 400°F. Layer a flat sheet with baking paper.

2. Section sweet potatoes in halves lengthwise, then slice each

half into thin pieces.

3. Transfer to the prepped sheet and heat for 20 minutes.

4. Drizzle with maple syrup and enjoy!

Turkey Sausage Patties

Total Prep and Cooking Time: 35 minutes

Makes: 4 Helpings

Protein: 11g

Carbohydrates: 2g

Fat: 8g

Sodium: 179g

Fiber: 0g

Calories: 121

What you need:

- ½ lb. ground turkey
- ¼ tsp. iodized salt
- ½ tsp. sage seasoning
- 1 tbsp. extra virgin olive oil
- ½ tsp. rosemary seasoning
- ⅛ tsp. black pepper
- ½ tbsp. pure maple syrup

Steps:

1. Use a glass dish to combine ground turkey, salt, sage, rosemary, black pepper, and maple syrup until incorporated.

2. Heat olive oil in a large skillet on your stove's medium heat setting.

3. Form 4 evenly sized patties and arrange in the pan, then cook in batches if necessary, as you want to leave some space in between to cook evenly.

4. Heat for approximately 6 minutes, then flip to the other side. Continue to brown for an additional 6 minutes or until cooked fully.

5. Transfer patties to a plate lined with kitchen paper to remove any excess grease.

6. Enjoy immediately!

Chapter Five:
Vegetarian Recipes

Cobb Tofu Salad

Total Prep and Cooking Time: 20 minutes

Makes: 4 Helpings

Protein: 11g

Carbohydrates: 9g

Fat: 16g

Sodium: 306g

Fiber: 6g

Calories: 203

What you need:

- ¼ tsp. turmeric powder
- 1 tbsp. garlic infused olive oil*
- ½ tsp. black pepper, separated
- 2 cups romaine lettuce, chopped
- ¼ tsp. kala namak (black salt)
- 8 oz. pre-pressed tofu, extra-firm and drained
- 2 tsp. lemon juice

- ¼ tsp. iodized salt

- 2 cups iceberg lettuce, chopped

- 1 cup avocado, sliced

- 2 tbsp. chives, chopped

- 1 cup cucumber, sliced

Steps:

1. Remove the shell of the avocado and section into wedges. Set aside.

2. Wash both iceberg and romaine lettuces well and chop into small sections together. Set aside with the avocado.

3. Scrub cucumber and chop into half lengthwise. Then, create thin sections and set aside with the other chopped vegetables.

4. Whisk ¼ teaspoon of black pepper along with kala namak and turmeric until incorporated in a glass dish.

5. Warm garlic-infused olive oil in a skillet and divide tofu into small sections in the pan.

6. Heat for about 10 minutes while tossing occasionally.

7. In the meantime, prepare salad dish with chopped vegetables.

8. Toss tofu with lemon juice and coat with the seasoning mixture. Transfer to the salad dish and season with the leftover ¼ teaspoon of black pepper, chives, and salt.

9. Serve with your favorite dressing and enjoy immediately!

* You can make your own homemade version of olive oil with the recipe found in chapter 13.

Corn and Carrot Fritters

Total Prep and Cooking Time: 25 minutes

Makes: 4 Helpings

Protein: 2g

Carbohydrates: 23g

Fat: 8g

Sodium: 179g

Fiber: 4g

Calories: 158

What you need:

- 2 bananas

- ¼ cup coconut milk, liquid

- ½ cup almond flour, blanched*

- ¼ tsp. iodized salt

- 2 large carrots

- ¼ cup chives, chopped finely

- 2 tbsp. parsley, chopped finely

- ¾ cup sweet corn, fresh or frozen

- 1 tbsp. extra virgin olive oil

- ¼ tsp. black pepper

Steps:

1. Scrub carrots thoroughly and use a kitchen grater to shred into smaller sections.

2. Use a glass dish to mash the banana, then blend milk and almond flour until integrated.

3. Combine salt, parsley, chives, carrots, black pepper, and corn until blended well.

4. Empty olive oil into a large skillet.

5. Once the pan is warm, distribute batter in small mounds. You will need to cook in batches, as you will have 12 in total.

6. Flatten mounds so they become small patties.

7. Warm for 3 minutes, then flip to the other side. Continue to heat for another 3 minutes or until your desired crispiness.

8. Remove to a kitchen paper-covered plate to drain any excess grease.

9. Repeat steps 5 through 8 for the remaining fritters. Make sure to add more olive oil as required.

10. Enjoy while still warm!

* You can also substitute homemade gluten-free flour with the recipe found in chapter 13.

Grilled Cheese Panini

Total Prep and Cooking Time: 20 minutes

Makes: 4 Sandwiches

Protein: 17g

Carbohydrates: 30g

Fat: 24g

Sodium: 650g

Fiber: 3g

Calories: 405

What you need:

- 8 slices gluten-free bread of your choice
- 1 cup basil leaves, loosely packed
- 1⅓ cup cheddar cheese, shredded
- 8 tsp. almond butter, unsalted
- 2 cups baby spinach, loosely packed
- ½ tsp. black pepper

Steps:

1. Apply almond butter on one side of each slice of bread.

2. Plug in the panini press to warm up properly.

3. Wash basil leaves and baby spinach well. Shake to remove extra water, then set aside.

4. Place one piece of bread with almond butter touching the hot grill.

5. Divide ingredients into quarters and layer basil leaves, cheddar cheese, black pepper, and baby spinach. Then, complete with a second piece of bread with almond butter facing the grill.

6. Close and heat for approximately 3 minutes. Transfer to a plate.

7. Repeat steps 4 through 6 for the additional 3 sandwiches.

8. Serve immediately and enjoy!

   If you do not own a panini press, you can also use a skillet. Create the sandwich, then place a saucepan on top. Turn the sandwich over after approximately 90 seconds, so you can properly brown both sides.

Quinoa Stuffed Acorn Squash

Total Prep and Cooking Time: 35 minutes

Makes: 4 Helpings

Protein: 8g

Carbohydrates: 51g

Fat: 9g

Sodium: 318g

Fiber: 7g

Calories: 300

What you need:

- 2 acorn squash

- 1⅔ tbsp. extra virgin olive oil, separated

- ½ tsp. iodized salt, separated

- 1 cup quinoa, uncooked and rinsed

- 2 cups water

- ½ cup parsley, chopped

- 2 cups spinach leaves

- 1 tbsp. lemon juice

- ½ tsp. black pepper, separated

Steps:

1. Set your stove to 375°F. Layer tin foil over a flat sheet and set aside.

2. Scrub acorn squash clean and slice into halves lengthwise. Remove the seeds and arrange on the prepped flat sheet.

3. Empty quinoa into a colander and run under cold water to rinse well. Leave in the sink to drain properly.

4. Drizzle with 1 tablespoon of olive oil and ¼ teaspoons, each of black pepper and salt.

5. Warm on the stove for 25 minutes.

6. In the meantime, use a saucepan on the highest heat setting to warm the water and quinoa.

7. As the water begins to bubble, enclose the pan and adjust heat to the lowest setting. Heat for a total of 15 minutes.

8. As the quinoa is being prepared, wash spinach thoroughly and shake to remove excess water. Transfer to a glass dish.

9. Combine the remaining ¼ teaspoons of black pepper and salt, leftover 2 teaspoons of olive oil, lemon juice, and parsley to the dish.

10. When quinoa has finished, transfer to a glass dish and toss all ingredients to combine fully.

11. Remove acorn squash from the stove and evenly distribute quinoa mix into the squash.

12. Enjoy immediately!

Chapter Six:
Seafood Recipes

Avocado and Shrimp

Total Prep and Cooking Time: 15 minutes

Makes: 4 Helpings

Protein: 12g

Carbohydrates: 4g

Fat: 21g

Sodium: 486g

Fiber: 3g

Calories: 250

What you need:

- 2 tbsp. coconut butter, unsalted

- ½ tsp. coriander seasoning

- 2 tbsp. garlic-infused olive oil*

- 12 oz. large shrimp

- 2 tsp. almond butter, unsalted

- 1 cup avocado, mashed

- ½ tsp. cumin seasoning

- 2 tsp. lime juice

Steps:

1. Peel and devein the shrimp. Make sure that they are dry by using a paper towel to remove extra moisture.

2. In a dish, mix coriander and cumin, then toss with the shrimp until they are coated.

3. Slice avocados in half and remove the seeds. Transfer meat to a separate dish and use a potato masher to crush.

4. Blend almond butter with avocado until incorporated. Transfer to a serving dish.

5. Warm a skillet with garlic-infused olive oil.

6. Toss shrimp into the skillet and wait about 90 seconds, then flip them over.

7. Remove with a slotted spoon to a serving plate with the avocado dip.

8. While the pan is still hot, distribute lime juice into the pan and add coconut butter.

9. Use a wooden spatula to scrape content off the pan, then distribute it on top of the shrimp.

10. Serve immediately with avocado dip and enjoy! * *You can make your own homemade version with the recipe found in chapter 13.*

Buttery Cod Fillet

Total Prep and Cooking Time: 15 minutes

Makes: 4 Helpings

Protein: 26g

Carbohydrates: 0g

Fat: 18g

Sodium: 809g

Fiber: 0g

Calories: 271

What you need:

- 1½ lbs. cod fillets

- ½ tsp. iodized salt

- 6 tbsp. almond butter, unsalted and separated

- 1 tbsp. lemon juice

- ¼ tsp. black pepper

Steps:

1. Rub black pepper and salt on both sides of the fish fillets.

2. Warm 2 tablespoons of almond butter in a non-stick skillet on a medium setting. Arrange fillets in the pan and cook in batches if needed.

3. Heat for 2 minutes, then turn over. Put leftover 4 tablespoons of almond butter on top of the fish and cook for an additional 4 minutes.

4. Drizzle lemon juice on fish and serve immediately. Enjoy!

Calamari Salad

Total Prep and Cooking Time:
10 minutes

Makes: 4 Helpings

Protein: 22g

Carbohydrates: 7g

Fat: 24g

Sodium: 639g

Fiber: 2g

Calories: 330

What you need:

- ½ tsp. lime juice

- 1 lb. calamari, sliced

- 3 tbsp. garlic-infused olive oil*

- 8 oz. olives, your preference

- 1 tbsp. coconut oil

- ⅛ tsp. black pepper

- ½ tsp. lemon juice

- 1 small head of romaine lettuce

Steps:

1. Thoroughly rinse lettuce and shake to remove any extra moisture.

2. Roughly chop into smaller sections and transfer to a serving dish. Set aside.

3. In a glass dish, combine garlic-infused olive oil and black pepper until integrated.

4. Use a non-stick skillet to liquefy coconut oil with olives.

5. Warm olives for approximately 90 seconds, then transfer to a serving plate with a slotted spoon.

6. Distribute sliced calamari in garlic-infused olive oil and seasonings.

7. Transfer calamari to the hot oil and heat for about 2 minutes or until they have a cloudy color.

8. Distribute to lettuce dish with olives and drizzle lemon and lime juice on top of the dish. Toss to combine fully.

9. Enjoy immediately!

   * *You can make your own homemade version with the recipe found in chapter 13.*

Coconut Crusted Fish

Total Prep and Cooking Time: 20 minutes

Makes: 4 Helpings

Protein: 22g

Carbohydrates: 3g

Fat: 15g

Sodium: 452g

Fiber: 1g

Calories: 229

What you need:

- ¼ cup coconut, shredded and unsweetened

- 2 tbsp. garlic infused olive oil, separated*

- zest from 2 limes

- ½ cup water

- 1 lb. white fish of choice (Pollack, Coley, Haddock or Cod)

- ½ cup Cheddar cheese, grated

Steps:

1. Apply ½ tablespoons of garlic infused olive oil to a rimmed flat sheet with a pastry brush and set aside.

2. Empty coconut and water into a glass dish. Set aside for 10

85

minutes.

3. In the meantime, zest limes, then set aside.

4. Adjust the oven to its grill setting.

5. Warm ½ tablespoon of garlic-infused olive oil in a large, non-stick skillet.

6. Arrange 2 fillets of fish in the pan and heat for 2 minutes. Turn to the other side and heat for another 2 minutes, then transfer to the prepared baking tray.

7. Repeat steps 5 and 6.

8. When ready, drain the water from the coconut using a colander and keep in the sink to drain properly.

9. As you are finishing the second batch of fish, heat the leftover ½ tablespoons of garlic-infused olive oil in an additional small skillet. Transfer lime zest.

10. Warm for about 90 seconds.

11. Transfer drained coconut to the pan and toss frequently for 60 seconds.

12. Top fish fillets with cheddar cheese and apply a coat of coconut crust to each.

13. Heat on the stove for approximately 90 seconds or until the crust starts to brown.

14. Remove from the stove carefully and enjoy immediately while hot.

You can make your own homemade version with the recipe found in chapter 13.

Cod Bites

Total Prep and Cooking Time:
20 minutes

Makes: 4 Helpings

Protein: 20g

Carbohydrates: 2g

Fat: 10g

Sodium: 675g

Fiber: 0g

Calories: 180

What you need:

- 2 cod fish

- ½ cup almond flour, blanched*

- ⅓ cup Parmesan cheese, grated

- 2 tbsp. garlic infused olive oil, separated**

- ⅛ tsp. black pepper

- 1 tsp. dill, chopped roughly

- ⅛ cup almond milk, unsweetened

- 1 tbsp. lemon juice

- ½ tsp. iodized salt, separated

Steps:

1. Preheat your oven to 400°F. Coat a flat pan with a tablespoon of garlic-infused olive oil and set aside.

2. Slice cod in fillets, then move to a plate layered with paper towels.

3. Cover fillets with another layer of paper towels and press to dry. Dust with ¼ teaspoon of salt and set aside.

4. In a food blender, pulse Parmesan cheese, black pepper, and the leftover ¼ teaspoon of salt until blended.

5. Combine chopped dill and almond flour and blend until incorporated.

6. Pour almond milk into a shallow dish and immerse each fillet into the liquid on both sides.

7. Then, cover fillets with the cheese mixture and place on the prepared flat sheet while leaving space in between.

8. Drizzle with the leftover tablespoon of garlic-infused olive oil and sprinkle the leftover cheese mixture on top.

9. Place sheet on the middle rack. Warm for 12 minutes, then carefully remove from the oven.

10. Drizzle with lemon juice and enjoy immediately!

* You can also substitute homemade gluten-free flour with the recipe found in chapter 13.

** You can make your own homemade version with the recipe found in chapter 13.

Salmon Skewers

Total Prep and Cooking Time:
30 minutes

Makes: 4 Helpings

Protein: 20g

Carbohydrates: 7g

Fat: 10g

Sodium: 263g

Fiber: 0g

Calories: 206

What you need:

- 14 oz. salmon fillets, boneless and skinless

- 2 tsp. garlic infused olive oil*

- 1½ tbsp. pure maple syrup

- 1 tbsp. lime juice

- zest from 1 lime

- 1½ tsp. ginger root, crushed

- 2 tbsp. gluten-free soy sauce**

- 1 cup water

- ½ tbsp. extra virgin olive oil

Steps:

1. Slice salmon fillets into bite-sized cubes.

2. Use a glass dish to blend soy sauce, lime zest and juice, maple syrup, ginger, and garlic-infused olive oil.

3. Transfer salmon cubes into the liquid and marinade for 10 minutes.

4. In the meantime, place 4 skewers in an additional glass dish with the water.

5. Prepare a rimmed flat sheet with olive oil by coating fully with a pastry brush. Set aside.

6. Adjust your oven to grill setting.

7. When the salmon is ready, remove with a slotted spoon to a plate and keep the marinade to the side.

8. Divide cubes evenly between skewers and arrange on the prepared flat sheet, so they are not touching.

9. Coat each piece of meat with marinade using a pastry brush.

10. Heat for a total of 9 minutes and turn skewers every 3 minutes while applying a new coat of marinade to each.

11. Remove from the oven and enjoy while it's hot!

*   You can make your own homemade version with the recipe found in chapter 13.*

**   If you are not able to find gluten-free soy sauce, tamari is a great gluten-free substitute.*

Shrimp Risotto

Total Prep and Cooking Time:
30 minutes

Makes: 4 Helpings

Protein: 19g

Carbohydrates: 48g

Fat: 15g

Sodium: 782g

Fiber: 2g

Calories: 403

What you need:

- ¼ cup almond milk, unsweetened

- 3 tbsp. garlic infused olive oil, separated*

- 1¼ cup risotto rice

- 2 cups chicken broth**

- ¼ cup dry white wine

- 1 tbsp. lemon juice

- ½ cup basil leaves, chopped and separated

- 12 oz. large shrimp, peeled and deveined

- ¼ cup Parmesan cheese, grated

91

Steps:

1. Rinse basil leaves and shake to remove any extra water. Chop roughly into smaller sections.

2. Empty 2 tablespoons of garlic-infused olive oil in a skillet over medium heat setting and warm ¼ cup of basil leaves for 90 seconds.

3. Blend rice in the skillet and toss occasionally for 3 minutes.

4. Distribute white wine and almond milk toss occasionally until liquid evaporates.

5. Add chicken broth and continue to heat until liquid is absorbed.

6. Empty the leftover garlic-infused olive oil in another skillet and add shrimp. Toss occasionally for 4 additional minutes.

7. Dust with black pepper and lemon juice.

* You can make your own homemade version with the recipe found in chapter 13.

** You can also use vegetable stock powder as a substitute found in chapter 13.

Shrimp Zoodles

Total Prep and Cooking Time:
25 minutes

Makes: 4 Helpings

Protein: 23g

Carbohydrates: 0g

Fat: 4g

Sodium: 281g

Fiber: 0g

Calories: 130

What you need:

- 1 tbsp. extra virgin olive oil

- ¼ tsp. black pepper

- 1 lb. shrimp, peeled and tails removed

- ¼ tsp. iodized salt

- 4 medium zucchinis

Steps:

1. Scrub zucchinis and use a julienne peeler to create spiral noodles out of each. Set aside in a dish.

2. Empty olive oil in a skillet on medium heat setting. Arrange shrimp in a single layer in the pan.

3. Dust with black pepper and salt and heat for 2 minutes.

4. Use a slotted spoon to remove shrimp to a plate. Set aside.

5. Transfer zoodles into the skillet and heat for 5 minutes while tossing frequently.

6. Distribute shrimp back into the pan and toss to combine. Heat for approximately 5 additional minutes or until shrimp are opaque.

7. Serve immediately while hot and enjoy!

* You can also use pesto, found in chapter 13, in this recipe for a variety in flavor. You would simply add ½ – 1 cup of pesto into the pan in step 6.

Smoked Haddock

Total Prep and Cooking Time: 15 minutes

Makes: 4 Helpings

Protein: 22g

Carbohydrates: 0g

Fat: 6g

Sodium: 657g

Fiber: 0g

Calories: 145

What you need:

- 12 oz. smoked haddock

- ¼ cup parsley, chopped

- 1½ tbsp. garlic-infused olive oil*

- 4½ cups water

- ¼ tsp. black pepper

Steps:

1. Boil water in a saucepan until it starts to bubble.

2. In the meantime, arrange haddock in a large skillet.

3. Empty the boiling water over fish and turn the burner on its lowest setting.

4. Poach for 10 minutes, then remove to a serving platter.

5. While fish is poaching, wash parsley and shake to remove extra water. Then, chop roughly and set aside.

6. Top the fish with garlic-infused olive oil, black pepper, and parsley and enjoy immediately!

* You can make your own homemade version with the recipe found in chapter 13.

Sweet and Tangy Trout

Total Prep and Cooking Time: 20 minutes

Makes: 4 Helpings

Protein: 24g

Carbohydrates: 12g

Fat: 16g

Sodium: 166g

Fiber: 1g

Calories: 290

What you need:

- 1 lb. Rainbow trout fillets
- 3½ tbsp. extra virgin olive oil, separated
- 2 tsp. black pepper
- 3 tbsp. pure maple syrup
- 1 tsp. ginger root, grated
- 3 tbsp. Dijon mustard

Steps:

1. Use a glass dish to blend black pepper, ginger, Dijon mustard, maple syrup, and leftover 3 tablespoons of olive oil. Set aside for 10 minutes.

2. Set your oven to 400°F.

3. Prepare a rimmed, flat sheet layered with tin foil. Use a pastry brush to apply ½ a tablespoon of olive oil to the tin foil.

4. Arrange trout fillets on the flat sheet.

5. When ready, spoon the sauce liberally over each fillet.

6. Measure the thickest area of the fish and heat 10 minutes for each inch.

7. Remove from the oven and serve immediately. You can store leftovers for up to 3 days.

* You will know that the fish is completely cooked when the thickest area has turned opaque pink. If it is still bright pink after cooking, continue to heat for 2 to 3 minutes.

** You can also substitute salmon in this recipe for rainbow trout.

Chapter Seven:
Poultry Recipes

Avocado Chicken Salad

Total Prep and Cooking Time: 15 minutes

Makes: 4 Helpings

Protein: 20g

Carbohydrates: 4g

Fat: 12g

Sodium: 598g

Fiber: 3g

Calories: 206

What you need:

- 12 oz. canned chicken, drained and shredded
- 1 cup avocado
- ¼ tsp. iodized salt
- 1 cup celery, chopped
- ⅛ tsp. black pepper
- 1 cup cilantro, chopped

Steps:

1. Remove the shell of the avocado and take out the seed. Pulse the avocado using a food blender for about 30 seconds.

2. Combine salt, chopped cilantro, chopped celery, chicken, and black pepper. Pulse for an additional 60 seconds until integrated.

3. Enjoy immediately.

Bacon Chicken Wrap

Total Prep and Cooking Time: 20 minutes

Makes: 4 Helpings

Protein: 17g

Carbohydrates: 11g

Fat: 13g

Sodium: 563g

Fiber: 3g

Calories: 225

What you need:

- 1 large head iceberg lettuce
- 4 tbsp. favorite dressing*
- 12 oz. chicken breast, deli or canned
- 8 strips bacon, turkey or pork
- ¼ tsp. black pepper, separated
- 1 tbsp. garlic-infused olive oil**

Steps:

1. Use a skillet to warm garlic-infused olive oil. Arrange bacon in the pan in a single layer and dust with black pepper.

101

2. Heat for approximately 7 minutes or until your desired level of crispiness.

3. Transfer to a plate layered with kitchen paper to remove any extra grease.

4. Lay out 4 sections of baking lining. Arrange 6 pieces of lettuce into the center of each, about 10 inches in length.

5. Equally divide the dressing between each and spread in the middle.

6. Layer turkey and bacon on top of the dressing.

7. Start rotating lettuce over the filling, folding in the edges as you roll. Use parchment paper to help keep it in place as you rotate the wrap.

8. Serve immediately and enjoy!

You can make your own homemade sauce in your kitchen with recipes found in chapter 13.

You can make your own homemade version with the recipe found in chapter 13.

Baked Lemon Pepper Chicken

Total Prep and Cooking Time: 30 minutes

Makes: 4 Tablespoons

Protein: 53g

Carbohydrates: 0g

Fat: 18g

Sodium: 129g

Fiber: 0g

Calories: 386

What you need:

- 4 chicken breast fillets, boneless and skinless

- 1 tbsp. lemon pepper seasoning*

- ¼ cup almond butter, unsalted

Steps:

1. Set your oven to 400°F. Prepare a glass baking dish with a layer of tin foil.

2. Transfer almond butter to the pan and allow it to liquefy in the oven.

3. In the meantime, rub each side of the chicken with lemon pepper seasoning.

4. Remove the pan from the oven and arrange the chicken inside. Enclose with an additional layer of tin foil.

5. Heat for 10 minutes, then turn the chicken breasts over. Continue to heat for an additional 10 minutes.

6. Carefully remove from the oven and serve immediately with a side of your choice. Enjoy!

* *You can make your own with the recipe found in chapter 13.*

Creamy Turkey and Carrots

Total Prep and Cooking Time:
20 minutes

Makes: 4 Helpings

Protein: 22g

Carbohydrates: 4g

Fat: 22g

Sodium: 570g

Fiber: 1g

Calories: 299

What you need:

- ¾ tsp. iodized salt

- 1 lb. ground turkey, lean

- ¾ tsp. black pepper

- 2 tbsp. coconut oil

- ¾ tsp. thyme seasoning

- 1 cup coconut milk, liquid

- ¾ tsp. celery salt

- 1 cup carrots, chopped

- ¾ tbsp. yellow mustard

Steps:

1. Dissolve coconut oil in a saucepan on medium/high heat.

2. Warm ground turkey in the saucepan and brown for approximately 7 minutes, stirring occasionally with a wooden scraper to break up the meat into small sections.

3. In the meantime, scrub carrots and remove the skins. Chop into small sections and transfer to the saucepan.

4. Blend salt, thyme, celery salt, mustard, and black pepper with the meat until fully integrated.

5. Turn the burner down and finally combine coconut milk into the pot. Simmer for about 6 additional minutes.

6. Serve hot and enjoy!

* You can substitute beef, lamb, or ground pork into this recipe as well.

Maple Mustard Chicken

Total Prep and Cooking Time:
35 minutes

Makes: 4 Helpings

Protein: 32g

Carbohydrates: 8g

Fat: 38g

Sodium: 358g

Fiber: 0g

Calories: 506

What you need:

- 4 chicken thighs, skin and bone included

- ⅓ tsp. black pepper

- 4 tsp. Dijon mustard

- 2 tbsp. pure maple syrup

- 1⅔ tbsp. extra virgin olive oil, separated

- 2 tsp. lemon juice

- ¼ tsp. iodized salt

Steps:

1. Set your oven to 400°F. Use 1 tablespoon of olive oil to grease the inside of a baking dish, then set aside.

2. Combine leftover ⅔ tablespoons of olive oil, lemon juice, maple syrup, and Dijon mustard in a glass dish until a smooth consistency, then set aside.

3. Slice 4 small gashes into the chicken skin and dust with black pepper and salt.

4. Arrange chicken skin facing up on the prepared baking dish and spoon sauce evenly over each piece.

5. Heat for a total of 25 minutes or until it hits an internal temperature of 165°F.

6. Carefully remove the dish from the oven and allow it to cool for 5 minutes before serving warm. Enjoy!

Sweet and Sour Chicken Celery Sticks

Total Prep and Cooking Time:
10 minutes

Makes: 4 Helpings

Protein: 22g

Carbohydrates: 11g

Fat: 13g

Sodium: 328g

Fiber: 1g

Calories: 258

What you need:

- ⅛ cup extra virgin olive oil

- 2 cups canned chicken, drained and shredded

- 3 tbsp. maple mustard sauce*

- ¾ tsp. iodized salt

- 6 medium celery stalks

- ¾ tsp. black pepper

- 1½ tbsp. chives, chopped

Steps:

1. Using a glass dish, blend olive oil, salt, maple mustard sauce, and black pepper until incorporated.

2. Combine chicken and stir thoroughly.

3. Cut celery stalks in halves.

4. Spoon chicken filling inside and garnish with chives.

5. Serve and enjoy!

   * You can find the recipe for homemade maple mustard sauce in chapter 13.

Turkey Burger Patties

Total Prep and Cooking Time: 20 minutes

Makes: 4 Helpings

Protein: 11g

Carbohydrates: 0g

Fat: 8g

Sodium: 185g

Fiber: 0g

Calories: 116

What you need:

- ½ tsp oregano seasoning
- 3 tsp. garlic-infused olive oil*
- ½ tsp. basil seasoning
- 1 cup zucchini, grated
- ¼ tsp. iodized salt
- 8 oz. ground turkey, lean
- ⅛ tsp. black pepper
- 1 tsp. parsley seasoning

Steps:

1. Scrub zucchini thoroughly and use a kitchen grater to shred using the largest holes available.

2. Use a dish to combine oregano, basil, zucchini, ground turkey, salt, parsley, and black pepper by hand until completely combined.

3. Section meat into 4 equal portions and use your hands to create flattened patties.

4. Warm garlic-infused olive oil in a large skillet. Once the skillet is hot, arrange the patties and heat for about 5 minutes, then turn over to the other side.

5. Brown for an additional 5 minutes until cooked fully through.

6. Serve warm with gluten-free buns or plain. Enjoy!

* You can make your own homemade version with the recipe found in chapter 13.

Chapter Eight:
Beef Recipes

Beef Stir Fry

Total Prep and Cooking Time:
30 minutes

Makes: 8 Helpings

Protein: 31g

Carbohydrates: 2g

Fat: 14g

Sodium: 229g

Fiber: 1g

Calories: 261

What you need:

- 1 lb beef strips, lean

- 1 tsp. coconut oil

- 1 small head lettuce, chopped

- 3 tbsp. coconut aminos

- 1 tsp ginger root, grated

- 1 medium carrot, sliced

- 1 medium zucchini, sliced

- ¼ tsp. iodized salt

Steps:

1. Rinse lettuce and shake to remove any extra water. Slice into thin sections and set aside.

2. Scrub zucchini and carrot, and slice into small sections. Set aside together.

3. Empty coconut oil in a large skillet and warm until liquefied.

4. Brown beef for 5 minutes while tossing occasionally.

5. Blend lettuce, ginger, and coconut aminos to the skillet and heat for an additional 2 minutes while tossing frequently. Then, turn the burner off.

6. Combine zucchini and carrot bits and toss to blend. Enclose the skillet with a cover, then steam for 3 minutes.

7. Remove the lid and dust with salt. Enjoy while it's hot.

Creamy Beef Strips

Total Prep and Cooking Time: 20 minutes

Makes: 4 Helpings

Protein: 28g

Carbohydrates: 2g

Fat: 7g

Sodium: 102g

Fiber: 1g

Calories: 183

What you need:

- 1 tsp. garlic-infused olive oil*

- 2 tsp. extra virgin olive oil

- 4 tsp. almond flour**

- 1 cup lettuce, sliced thinly

- 3 tbsp. canned coconut milk, chilled

- 1 lb. beef strips, lean

- 2 tsp. Dijon mustard

- 1 cup water

- ¾ cup parsley, chopped roughly

Steps:

1. Wash lettuce and shake to remove any extra water. Chop into small sections and set aside.

2. Warm the pan with extra virgin olive oil and garlic-infused olive oil at medium/high setting.

3. Brown chopped lettuce for about 90 seconds, then transfer it to a glass dish with a slotted spoon.

4. Next, brown meat while tossing occasionally for approximately 6 minutes.

5. Distribute almond flour into the pan and toss frequently for about 60 seconds.

6. Blend Dijon mustard and water to the pan and adjust the heat to the lowest setting, so sauce can thicken.

7. Once sauce has reduced to your desired thickness, turn the burner off.

8. Distribute liquid from the canned coconut milk into a lidded container for use later in another recipe.   .

9. Integrate 3 tablespoons of solid coconut milk into the dish and toss to combine fully.

10. Top with chopped parsley and serve immediately.

* You can make your own homemade version with the recipe found in chapter 13.

** You can also substitute homemade gluten-free flour with the recipe found in chapter 13.

Flat Iron Steak

Total Prep and Cooking Time: 15 minutes

Makes: 4 Helpings

Protein: 15g

Carbohydrates: 1g

Fat: 15g

Sodium: 263g

Fiber: 0g

Calories: 295

What you need:

- 12 oz. flat iron steaks, lean

- ¼ tsp. iodized salt, separated

- 4 tsp. extra virgin olive oil, separated

- ¼ cup black olives, drained and pitted

- 1 tsp. garlic-infused olive oil*

- ⅛ cup capers, drained

- 2 tsp. fresh thyme leaves

- ¼ tsp. black pepper, separated

Steps:

1. Use a food blender to pulse olives, garlic-infused olive oil, capers, and thyme leaves for approximately 2 minutes or until the consistency is a paste.

2. Arrange steaks on a cutting board and drizzle with 2 teaspoons of olive oil.

3. Dust each one with ⅛ teaspoon of black pepper and salt.

4. Place meat on a grill and warm for approximately 4 minutes on each side.*

5. Remove from heat to a section of tin foil. Enclose and wait 5 minutes before transferring to a serving platter.

6. Transfer paste to a serving dish and use a topping or dip for the steak. Enjoy!

You can make your own homemade version with the recipe found in chapter 13.

This recipe is for medium rare steaks. *If you like your steaks rare, only cook 2 minutes on each side and for medium well, increase to 6 minutes each side.*

Teriyaki Beef Skewers

Total Prep and Cooking Time:
30 minutes

Makes: 4 Helpings

Protein: 25g

Carbohydrates: 3g

Fat: 9g

Sodium: 564g

Fiber: 0g

Calories: 189

What you need:

- 1 lb. beef mince, lean

- 4 tbsp. gluten-free teriyaki sauce, low sodium

- 1¼ tsp. black pepper, separated

- 2 tsp. garlic-infused olive oil*

- ¼ tsp. iodized salt

- 1 cup water

119

Steps:

1. Use a glass dish to combine 1 teaspoon of black pepper along with teriyaki sauce and minced meat.

2. Use your hands to mold meat into 20 small spheres. Place on 4 individual metal skewers.

3. Arrange on a serving platter and cover with a layer of plastic wrap. Refrigerate for 15 minutes.

4. Preheat the grill or barbecue and remove the skewers from the fridge.

5. Arrange on the grill and heat for approximately 6 minutes on each side. You will know they are done when juice from the meat is clear.

6. Enjoy immediately!

  * You can make your own homemade version with the recipe found in chapter 13.

Veggie Steak Plate

Total Prep and Cooking Time: 20 minutes

Makes: 4 Helpings

Protein: 17g

Carbohydrates: 0g

Fat: 9g

Sodium: 214g

Fiber: 0g

Calories: 155

What you need:

- ¼ lb. sirloin steak, approximately 1 inch thick

- 2 tbsp. garlic-infused olive oil, separated*

- ¼ tsp. iodized salt, separated

- 2 cups zucchini, chopped

- ¼ tsp. black pepper, separated

- 1 cup carrots, chopped

121

Steps:

1. Set your oven to broil. Set a flat sheet with a rim inside to heat.

2. Pat excess moisture from the meat and sprinkle with season with ⅛ teaspoon of salt and pepper.

3. Scrub zucchinis and carrots and roughly chop together in small chunks.

4. Toss zucchini and carrot bits in 1½ tablespoons of garlic-infused olive oil and the remaining ⅛ teaspoons of black pepper and salt; ensure they are fully coated.

5. Remove the pan from the oven and brush with the remaining ½ tablespoon of garlic-infused olive oil in the center of the pan.

6. Place meat on the oil and arrange vegetables around the meat.

7. Heat for about 5 minutes and turn the meat to the other side. Toss the vegetables.

8. Broil for another 5 minutes, then place the pan on the stove top.

9. Transfer to a serving platter and enjoy immediately while hot.

* You can make your own homemade version with the recipe found in chapter 13.

Chapter Nine:
Lamb Dish Recipes

Lamb and Sweet Potato Fritters

Total Prep and Cooking Time: 35 minutes

Makes: 4 Helpings

Protein: 25g

Carbohydrates: 15g

Fat: 21g

Sodium: 273g

Fiber: 2g

Calories: 344

What you need:

- 1 tbsp. extra virgin olive oil, separated

- 2 large sweet potatoes

- 1 tbsp. garlic-infused olive oil*

- 5 tsp. gluten-free soy sauce**

- 1 tbsp. ginger root, crushed

- ¼ tsp. gluten-free Worcestershire sauce

- 1 cup cilantro, chopped

- 5 cups water

- 1 lb. ground lamb, lean

Steps:

1. Set your oven to 350°F and place a flat sheet layered with baking paper aside.

2. Empty water into a deep saucepan and allow it to bubble.

3. In the meantime, scrub sweet potatoes and remove the skins. Chop into small cubes and transfer to pot with bubbling water, then heat for a total of 10 minutes or until soft.

4. As the sweet potatoes are cooking, empty garlic-infused olive oil into a large skillet.

5. Brown lamb meat for approximately 4 minutes before tossing with a wooden spatula to break apart into smaller sections.

6. Blend cilantro, Worcestershire sauce, soy sauce, and ginger into the skillet. Toss to combine and heat for a couple of minutes longer.

7. Remove water from the sweet potatoes with a colander and transfer to a glass dish. Use a potato masher to crush.

8. Use a slotted spoon to transfer meat mix to the glass dish. Incorporate fully.

9. Equally divide fritters into patties and arrange on the prepped sheet.

10. Apply ½ tablespoon of olive oil to each using a pastry brush

and transfer to the oven.

11. Heat for 10 minutes and remove to the stove top.

12. Flip each patty over and apply the remaining ½ tablespoon of olive oil to the top of each fritter. Continue to brown for 10 additional minutes.

13. Remove from the stove and wait about 5 minutes before serving. Enjoy!

* You can make your own homemade version with the recipe found in chapter 13.

** If you are not able to find gluten-free soy sauce, tamari is a great gluten-free substitute.

Lamb Chops

Total Prep and Cooking Time:
20 minutes

Makes: 4 Helpings

Protein: 39g

Carbohydrates: 0g

Fat: 10g

Sodium: 248g

Fiber: 0g

Calories: 256

What you need:

- ¼ tsp. black pepper

- 1 tbsp. garlic infused olive oil*

- 4 lamb shoulder chops

- ¼ tsp. iodized salt

Steps:

1. Warm garlic-infused olive oil in a large skillet.

2. In the meantime, dust each lamb chop with ⅛ teaspoons of black pepper and salt. Rub spices into the meat, then repeat on the other side.

3. Arrange lamb chops into the pan and cook in batches if necessary.

4. Heat for 4 minutes and flip to the other side. Continue to brown for 4 additional minutes.

5. Transfer to a plate covered with kitchen paper to remove any excess grease.

6. Wait approximately 5 minutes before serving. Enjoy!

* You can make your own homemade version with the recipe found in chapter 13.

Lamb with Lemon Sauce

Total Prep and Cooking Time:
20 minutes + 30-minute
minimum marinade time

Makes: 4 Helpings

Protein: 21g

Carbohydrates: 2g

Fat: 28g

Sodium: 122g

Fiber: 0g

Calories: 344

What you need:

- 12 oz. lamb cutlets

- 1 tbsp. lemon juice

- zest from one lemon

- 1⅓ tbsp. thyme, chopped

- ¼ cup extra virgin olive oil

- 1⅓ tbsp. Dijon mustard

Steps:

1. Blend thyme, Dijon mustard, olive oil, lemon juice, and zest in a glass dish.

2. Arrange lamb in a baking dish, in a single layer if possible.

3. Set aside for 30 minutes. If not completely covered, turn meat over occasionally.

4. Remove from marinade and arrange on the grill at medium heat.

5. Warm for 5 minutes on each side.

6. Wait 5 minutes before serving and enjoy!

Chapter Ten:
Pork Dish Recipes

Ham Mac and Cheese Casserole

Total Prep and Cooking Time: 30 minutes

Makes: 4 Helpings

Protein: 22g

Carbohydrates: 37g

Fat: 18g

Sodium: 528g

Fiber: 2g

Calories: 493

What you need:

- 1½ cups gluten-free macaroni pasta

- 1 tsp. oregano seasoning

- ¼ tsp. black pepper

- 1 cup Cheddar cheese, grated and separated

- 2⅓ tbsp. almond butter, unsalted

- 1½ cups ham, cubed

- 3 tbsp. almond flour*

- 2 cups almond milk, unsweetened

- ¼ tsp. iodized salt

- 3 cups water

Steps:

1. Set your oven to 350°F and set a glass baking dish aside.

2. Empty water into a saucepan and wait for it to start bubbling.

3. Transfer macaroni and heat for approximately 7 minutes or until al dente.

4. In the meantime, dissolve almond butter in a small skillet.

5. Blend oregano and flour in the almond butter and toss to combine fully.

6. Add almond milk to the skillet ½ cup at a time and toss with a whisk to ensure it is incorporated fully. The consistency should bc smooth.

7. Allow to bubble for 3 minutes as you are constantly whisking as the sauce thickens.

8. Blend black pepper, ½ cup of cheddar cheese, and salt into the sauce, and continue to toss for an additional minute.

9. When ready, remove water from the macaroni with a colander, then transfer macaroni to the baking dish.

10. Toss ham and sauce in with the macaroni until integrated.

11. Dust with the leftover ½ cup of cheddar cheese and heat for a

total of 15 minutes.

12. Serve immediately. Enjoy!

You can also substitute homemade gluten-free flour with the recipe found in chapter 13.

Herbed Meatballs

Total Prep and Cooking Time: 35 minutes

Makes: 4 Helpings

Protein: 34g

Carbohydrates: 22g

Fat: 30g

Sodium: 490g

Fiber: 2g

Calories: 500

What you need:

- 1 lb. ground pork
- ¼ tsp. iodized salt
- ¾ cup gluten-free breadcrumbs, plain
- 1 medium banana
- ½ tsp. rosemary seasoning
- ¾ tbsp. basil, chopped
- ¼ cup Parmesan cheese, grated finely
- ½ tsp. oregano seasoning
- ¼ tsp. black pepper
- 1 tbsp. garlic-infused olive oil**

Steps:

1. Adjust your oven to 400°F and layer tin foil over a flat sheet, then set the sheet aside.

2. Use a glass dish to blend ground pork, salt, breadcrumbs, banana, rosemary, basil, Parmesan cheese, oregano, and black pepper by hand until incorporated.

3. Roll into small spheres and arrange on the prepped flat sheet. Drizzle with garlic-infused olive oil.

4. Heat in the oven for 13 minutes, then turn meatballs over and continue to heat for an additional 13 minutes or until the internal temperature of the meatballs reaches 160°F.

5. Remove from the oven and enjoy immediately over zoodles or as is.

* You are able to make these ahead of time and freeze them. After letting them cool down, transfer them to a flat sheet lined with a section of a baking sheet while leaving an inch in between each meatball. Transfer to the freezer overnight. You can then transfer them to a freezer-safe bag or container. When ready to eat, you would simply arrange them on a flat sheet and heat in the oven at 375°F. They will stay fresh in the freezer for up to 2 months.

** You can make your own homemade version with the recipe found in chapter 13.

Maple Ham

Total Prep and Cooking Time:
20 minutes

Makes: 4 Helpings

Protein: 15g

Carbohydrates: 24g

Fat: 2g

Sodium: 813g

Fiber: 0g

Calories: 172

What you need:

- 12 oz. deli ham

- 1 tbsp. pure maple syrup

- 1 tbsp. Dijon mustard

- ¼ cup brown sugar, firmly packed

- 1 tbsp. lemon juice

Steps:

1. Set your oven to 350°F and layer a flat sheet with a rim with tin foil. Set the sheet aside.

2. In a glass dish, combine maple syrup, Dijon mustard, brown sugar, and lemon juice until integrated fully. It should become a thick sauce.

3. Immerse slices of ham in the sauce and arrange on the prepped flat sheet.

4. Empty the leftover sauce over top of the ham.

5. Heat for a total of 15 minutes and enjoy immediately.

Pineapple Pork

Total Prep and Cooking Time:
15 minutes + overnight marinating

Makes: 4 Helpings

Protein: 42g

Carbohydrates: 15g

Fat: 9g

Sodium: 129g

Fiber: 0g

Calories: 215

What you need:

- 4 pork chops, boneless

- 2 tbsp. pure maple syrup

- 2 tsp. garlic-infused olive oil*

- ¾ tsp. nutmeg powder

- 2 tsp. thyme seasoning

- 1 cup pineapple juice, natural and unsweetened

Steps:

1. In a glass baking dish, blend maple syrup, garlic-infused olive oil, nutmeg, thyme, and pineapple juice.

2. Empty into a zip lock bag and insert pork chops and ensure the meat is fully covered.

3. Place in the refrigerator overnight to marinate.

4. When ready to prepare, remove the meat from the bag and arrange on a barbeque or griddle pan.

5. Heat the lamb chops for approximately 3 minutes on each side.

6. In the meantime, empty the marinade into a separate skillet on medium/high heat.

7. Transfer the meat to a serving platter and distribute the warmed marinade over top. Enjoy immediately!

  * *You can make your own homemade version with the recipe found in chapter 13.*

Pork and Rice

Total Prep and Cooking Time: 30 minutes

Makes: 4 Helpings

Protein: 20g

Carbohydrates: 12g

Fat: 7g

Sodium: 129g

Fiber: 1g

Calories: 200

What you need:

- 1 tbsp. garlic-infused olive oil*

- ¾ lbs. pork loin, boneless

- 1 cup quick cooking brown rice

- ¾ cup chicken broth, low sodium

- ½ tsp. ground turmeric

- ¼ tsp. thyme seasoning

- 1 lemon, sliced in quarters

Steps:

1. Slice pork lions into thin strips and set aside.

2. Warm garlic-infused olive oil in a large skillet on medium heat setting.

3. Arrange meat in the pan and toss occasionally for 8 minutes.

4. Transfer thyme, turmeric, broth, and brown rice to the skillet and toss to combine.

5. Allow liquid to start bubbling, then turn heat to the lowest setting.

6. Enclose the pan and warm for 12 minutes while tossing occasionally.

7. Remove the lid and continue to warm for an additional 5 minutes while tossing occasionally. The liquid should be mostly reduced by this point.

8. Transfer to a serving dish and serve with sliced lemons. Enjoy!

* You can make your own homemade version with the recipe found in chapter 13.

Sweet and Sour Pork

Total Prep and Cooking Time: 20 minutes

Makes: 4 Helpings

Protein: 37g

Carbohydrates: 8g

Fat: 17g

Sodium: 116g

Fiber: 1g

Calories: 445

What you need:

- 3 tbsp. almond flour*

- ½ tsp. black pepper

- 4 pork loin steaks, fat removed

- 2 tbsp. garlic-infused olive oil**

- ½ cup pineapple, chopped and unsweetened

- ½ cup pineapple juice, no added sugar

- 3 tbsp. lime juice

- ½ tsp. gluten-free soy sauce***

Steps:

1. In a small dish, blend black pepper and almond flour and set aside.

2. Arrange pork steaks between two sections of plastic wrap.

3. Use a meat mallet to beat the meat so it is half its original thickness, then set aside.

4. Use a food blender to pulse pineapple, pineapple juice, and lime juice until a slightly chunky consistency. Set aside.

5. Cover steaks in the flour mixture and shake to remove any extra batter.

6. Warm garlic-infused olive oil on a large skillet. Arrange steaks in the pan and cook in batches if necessary.

7. Heat for approximately 2 minutes on each side.

8. Distribute the sauce into the skillet and set to the lowest heat setting. Warm for 2 additional minutes.

9. Transfer the steak to a serving platter and top with sauce. Enjoy immediately!

* You can also substitute homemade gluten-free flour with the recipe found in chapter 13.

** You can make your own homemade version with the recipe found in chapter 13.

*** If you are not able to find gluten-free soy sauce, tamari is a great gluten-free substitute.

Chapter Eleven:
Vegetable and Side Recipes

Coleslaw Salad

Total Prep and Cooking Time: 10 minutes

Makes: 4 Helpings

Protein: 1g

Carbohydrates: 3g

Fat: 7g

Sodium: 35g

Fiber: 1g

Calories: 74

What you need:

- 1½ tsp. Dijon mustard

- 1 small head of lettuce

- ⅛ cup extra virgin olive oil

- 1½ tsp. lemon juice

- 1 large carrot, peeled

143

Steps:

1. Wash lettuce well and shake to remove any extra water. Use a kitchen grater on the side with the largest holes to shred the lettuce. Transfer to a large serving dish.

2. Scrub carrot and remove the skin with a vegetable peeler. Grate with a kitchen grater with the largest holes, then transfer to the serving dish.

3. In a glass dish, combine lemon juice, Dijon mustard, and olive oil until integrated.

4. Distribute over salad and toss to combine fully. Serve immediately and enjoy!

Cucumber Salad

Total Prep and Cooking Time: 10 minutes

Makes: 4 Helpings

Protein: 6g

Carbohydrates: 3g

Fat: 0g

Sodium: 21g

Fiber: 0g

Calories: 37

What you need:

- 1 large cucumber
- ½ cup chives, chopped
- 1 tsp. fresh dill
- 2 tbsp. white vinegar
- 1 cup canned coconut milk, chilled

145

Steps:

1. Scrub cucumber well and use a mandolin to slice to your desired thickness.

2. Remove the lid for the canned coconut milk and distribute the liquid to a lidded container for use in a different recipe.

3. Transfer to a glass dish and toss solid coconut milk, white vinegar, dill, and chives until the cucumbers are fully covered.

4. Serve immediately or refrigerate up to 2 days in a lidded container. Enjoy!

Garlic Croutons

Total Prep and Cooking Time: 10 minutes

Makes: 8 Helpings

Protein: 1g

Carbohydrates: 4g

Fat: 2g

Sodium: 37g

Fiber: 0g

Calories: 34

What you need:

- 2 slices gluten-free bread, stale

- 1 tbsp. garlic-infused olive oil*

Steps:

1. Remove crusts from the slices of bread, then slice into small cubes.

2. Heat garlic-infused olive oil in a skillet and toss the bread cubes constantly for approximately 3 minutes.

3. Transfer to a plate layered with kitchen paper and serve immediately. They will also keep fresh in a lidded container or plastic bag for up to one month.

You can make your own homemade version with the recipe found in chapter 13.

Glazed Edamame

Total Prep and Cooking Time: 15 minutes

Makes: 4 Helpings

Protein: 10g

Carbohydrates: 17g

Fat: 6g

Sodium: 590g

Fiber: 4g

Calories: 156

What you need:

- 2 cups edamame, not-shucked and frozen

- 4 tbsp. water, separated

- 2 tsp. garlic-infused olive oil*

- ¼ tsp. iodized salt

- 2 tbsp. pure maple syrup

- 1 tsp. ginger root, minced finely

- 4 tbsp. gluten-free soy sauce**

- 2 tbsp. rice vinegar

- 4 cups water

149

Steps:

1. Empty 4 cups of water in a deep pot with salt and heat until it starts to bubble.

2. Distribute edamame into the pot and boil for approximately 5 minutes.

3. Immediately remove the water with a colander and rinse under cool water.

4. In the meantime, blend maple syrup, ginger, rice vinegar, soy sauce, and the leftover 4 tablespoons of water in a glass dish until combined.

5. Warm garlic-infused olive oil in a skillet and distribute the mixture for 6 minutes as the sauce reduces.

6. Transfer the edamame to the glaze and toss to coat fully.

7. Serve immediately and enjoy!

* You can make your own homemade version with the recipe found in chapter 13.

** If you are not able to find gluten-free soy sauce, tamari is a great gluten-free substitute.

Pesto Pasta Salad

Total Prep and Cooking Time:
20 minutes

Makes: 4 Helpings

Protein: 5g

Carbohydrates: 45g

Fat: 16g

Sodium: 301g

Fiber: 1g

Calories: 349

What you need:

- ¼ tsp. black pepper

- 3½ cups arugula, separated

- 1½ cup mint leaves, separated

- ¼ tsp. iodized salt

- 7½ oz. brown rice noodles*

- ½ cup basil, chopped

- 3 qts. water

- 1 tbsp. extra virgin olive oil, separated

- 3 tbsp. garlic-infused olive oil**

- 2 tbsp. almond butter, unsalted

- 1 tbsp. lemon juice

Steps:

1. Empty water into a deep pot and allow it to bubble.

2. Transfer noodles to the water with 1 teaspoon of olive oil and heat for 8 minutes or until al dente.

3. In the meantime, rinse 3 cups of arugula and 1 cup of mint leaves and shake to remove any extra moisture.

4. Chop finely together and set aside.

5. Rinse the leftover ½ cup each of arugula, mint leaves, and basil, and chop into small sections, then transfer to a food blender.

6. Combine salt, lemon juice, almond butter, black pepper, and garlic-infused olive oil into a food blender and pulse until a smooth consistency.

7. When the noodles have finished cooking, remove water with a colander and rinse with cold water. Transfer to a serving platter.

8. Drizzle with the leftover 2 teaspoons of olive oil over the noodles.

9. Toss with the chopped mint, arugula, and pesto sauce and enjoy immediately.

You can also substitute any gluten-free pasta of your choice.

**You can make your own homemade version with the recipe found in chapter 13.*

Quinoa Salad

Total Prep and Cooking Time:
25 minutes

Makes: 4 Helpings

Protein: 8g

Carbohydrates: 23g

Fat: 14g

Sodium: 673g

Fiber: 7g

Calories: 237

What you need:

- 1 cup quinoa, uncooked
- 3 tbsp. gluten-free soy sauce*
- ½ tsp. toasted sesame oil
- 1 tbsp. garlic infused olive oil**
- ½ tsp. ginger root, grated
- 8 cups water
- ⅓ tsp. iodized salt
- 5 oz. baby spinach
- ⅓ cup almonds, unsalted and sliced

- 10 oz. carrots, grated

- ½ tbsp. lime juice

- ¼ black pepper

Steps:

1. Rinse quinoa under cold water. Distribute to a deep pot and combine salt and water with the quinoa.

2. Warm on the highest heat setting until water is bubbling. Turn the burner down to medium/low and warm for another 12 minutes or until fluid is fully reduced.

3. Meanwhile, wash ginger and carrots well. Use a kitchen grater to shred each completely.

4. Rinse spinach and shake to remove extra water. Set aside.

5. Warm garlic-infused olive oil, ginger, and soy sauce for approximately 60 seconds.

6. Blend spinach in the pan for about 5 minutes and turn the burner off.

7. Combine quinoa, black pepper, lime juice, toasted sesame oil, carrots, and almonds to the pan and incorporate fully.

8. Serve while hot and enjoy!

* If you are not able to find gluten-free soy sauce, tamari is a great gluten-free substitute.

** You can make your own homemade version with the recipe found in chapter 13.

Roasted Carrots

Total Prep and Cooking Time: 30 minutes

Makes: 4 Helpings

Protein: 2g

Carbohydrates: 17g

Fat: 14g

Sodium: 270g

Fiber: 5g

Calories: 194

What you need:

- ¼ tsp. black pepper

- 10 large carrots

- 1 tbsp. extra virgin olive oil

- ¼ tsp. iodized salt

Steps:

1. Set your oven to 400°F and place a flat sheet with a rim to the side.

2. Thoroughly scrub carrots and remove the ends of each. Use kitchen paper to remove any excess moisture.

3. Slice in half lengthwise and arrange on the prepped pan.

4. Drizzle with olive oil and dust with black pepper and salt.

5. Heat for 25 minutes. At about 12 mins 30 seconds, toss them to the other side.

6. Remove from the oven and serve immediately.

Roasted Zucchini

Total Prep and Cooking Time:
20 minutes

Makes: 4 Helpings

Protein: 0g

Carbohydrates: 0g

Fat: 14g

Sodium: 146g

Fiber: 0g

Calories: 121

What you need:

- 2 large zucchinis
- ¼ tsp. iodized salt, separated
- ⅓ cup extra virgin olive oil
- ¼ tsp. black pepper

Steps:

1. Set your oven to 400°F and set a flat sheet aside.

2. Scrub zucchinis thoroughly and slice the ends off. Slice into thin sections.

3. Arrange in a single layer on the flat sheet.

4. Dust the zucchini with salt and black pepper.

5. Drizzle with olive oil and heat for a total of 14 minutes.

6. Transfer to a serving dish and enjoy immediately.

Sautéed Zucchini

Total Prep and Cooking Time:
10 minutes

Makes: 4 Helpings

Protein: 0g

Carbohydrates: 1g

Fat: 3g

Sodium: 147g

Fiber: 0g

Calories: 33

What you need:

- 2 medium zucchinis, diagonally sliced

- ¼ tsp. black pepper

- 1 tbsp. extra virgin olive oil

- ½ tbsp. lemon juice

- 2 tbsp. parsley leaves, chopped

- ¼ tsp. iodized salt

Steps:

1. Scrub zucchinis and slice thinly on a diagonal. Set aside.

2. Empty olive oil into a skillet and warm over medium heat.

3. Toss occasionally for 6 minutes, then turn the burner off.

4. Blend black pepper, parsley, lemon zest, and salt into the skillet and toss to combine fully.

5. Serve immediately and enjoy!

Spinach Pasta

Total Prep and Cooking Time:
10 minutes

Makes: 4 Helpings

Protein: 8g

Carbohydrates: 47g

Fat: 7g

Sodium: 316g

Fiber: 3g

Calories: 280

What you need:

- 1 tbsp. garlic-infused olive oil, separated*

- 8 oz. spinach leaves

- ¼ tsp. black pepper

- 8 oz. brown rice pasta**

- ¼ tsp. iodized salt

- 8 cups water

- ¼ cup Parmesan cheese, grated

Steps:

1. Empty water and salt into a deep pot and wait until it starts to bubble.

2. Distribute noodles and heat for approximately 8 minutes or until al dente.

3. In the meantime, warm ½ a tablespoon of garlic-infused olive oil in a skillet.

4. Rinse spinach leaves and shake to remove excess moisture.

5. Transfer to the skillet and toss frequently for 2 minutes.

6. Remove water from the pasta with a colander and transfer to a serving dish.

7. Toss in spinach and Parmesan cheese and drizzle the leftover ½ tablespoon of garlic-infused olive oil.

8. Serve while hot and enjoy!

* You can make your own homemade version with the recipe found in chapter 13.

** You can also substitute any gluten-free pasta of your choice.

Vegetable Chips

Total Prep and Cooking Time:
30 minutes

Makes: 4 Helpings

Protein: 3g

Carbohydrates: 12g

Fat: 4g

Sodium: 328g

Fiber: 4g

Calories: 89

What you need:

- 1 medium sweet potato

- 1½ medium carrots

- 1 small turnip

- ½ tsp. iodized salt

- 1 medium zucchini

- ½ tsp. black pepper

- 1 tbsp. extra virgin olive oil

Steps:

1. Set your oven to 400°F. Use baking lining to layer a flat sheet with a rim.

2. Scrub the zucchini, turnip, and carrots, and use a mandolin to slice them thinly and uniformly to be approximately ¼ inch in width. Transfer all into a glass dish.

3. Blend black pepper, olive oil, and salt, completely covering the vegetables.

4. Arrange on the prepped pan without layering. Heat for 10 minutes, then turn them over.

5. Heat for approximately 8 more minutes, just before any of the sides start turning brown.

6. Wait about 5 minutes before serving and enjoy!

Chapter Twelve:
Snack and Sweet Treat Recipes

Butter Pecan Cookies

Total Prep and Cooking Time: 25 minutes

Makes: 8 Cookies

Protein: 1g

Carbohydrates: 16g

Fat: 13g

Sodium: 151g

Fiber: 1g

Calories: 127

What you need:

- ½ cup Stevia sweetener, granulated

- ½ cup almond butter, unsalted

- 1¾ cups almond flour, blanched*

- ½ cup pecans, chopped

- 2 tbsp. coconut flour

- ½ tsp. iodized salt

- ½ tsp. pure vanilla extract, sugar-free

Steps:

1. Adjust the oven to 325°F. Cover a flat sheet with baking paper and set aside.

2. Using a glass dish, cream sweetener, vanilla extract, and almond butter with an electric beater until it is a fluffy consistency.

3. Combine almond flour and coconut flour to the mixture until incorporated.

4. Carefully fold pecans and salt into the batter.

5. Scoop out the dough with a spoon or cookie scoop. Create 1-inch balls of dough and lightly press them approximately 2 inches from each other on the prepared flat sheet.

6. Heat in the oven for 5 minutes, then transfer the cookie sheet to the counter. Use a smooth bottomed glass to press each cookie about ¼ inch thick.

7. Heat in the oven for an additional 12 minutes.

8. Leave them to set on the cookie pan for approximately 10 minutes for them to set properly before enjoying.

* You can also substitute homemade gluten-free flour with the recipe found in chapter 13.

Cacao Peanut Balls

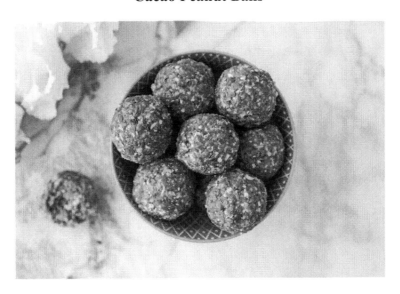

Total Prep and Cooking Time: 25 minutes

Makes: 4 Balls

Protein: 3g

Carbohydrates: 6g

Fat: 20g

Sodium: 3g

Fiber: 1g

Calories: 203

What you need:

- ¼ cup peanuts, raw and unsalted

- ⅓ cup coconut flour**

- ¼ cup almond butter, unsalted

- ⅛ cup powdered cacao, unsweetened

- ¼ cup coconut oil

Steps:

1. In a saucepan, liquefy almond butter and coconut oil until the mixture is a smooth consistency.

2. In a glass dish, blend cacao powder and coconut flour. Empty melted butter and combine completely.

3. Transfer to the freezer for 15 minutes so it can set.

4. Meanwhile, in a food blender, pulse peanuts for approximately 60 seconds until chopped.

5. Transfer to a plate.

6. Remove the dish from the freezer and divide the batter into 8 equal sections. Roll spheres by hand from each section.

7. Rotate the balls in peanuts and arrange on a serving platter.

8. Refrigerate for 5 minutes and serve. Enjoy!

* Any leftovers can be stored in a lidded container and will keep up to 7 days.

** You can also substitute homemade gluten-free flour with the recipe found in chapter 13.

Carrot Cake Bites

Total Prep and Cooking Time: 10 minutes

Makes: 4 Helpings

Protein: 2g

Carbohydrates: 11g

Fat: 9g

Sodium: 88g

Fiber: 2g

Calories: 111

What you need:

- 4 baby carrots, peeled and chopped

- ⅛ tsp. pure vanilla extract, sugar-free

- 2 tbsp. almond butter, unsalted

- ⅛ tsp. ground cinnamon

- ⅓ cup shredded coconut, unsweetened

- 1 tbsp. pure maple syrup

- ⅓ cup gluten-free rolled oats

- ⅛ tsp. iodized salt

Steps:

1. Thoroughly clean carrots and remove the skins. Chop into big chunks and transfer to a food blender.

2. Pulse for approximately 2 minutes until consistency is slightly chunky.

3. Transfer to a glass dish. Combine coconut and oats in a food blender and pulse for an additional 2 minutes.

4. Empty carrots, almond butter, maple syrup, salt, vanilla extract, and cinnamon in a food blender and pulse for a total of 2 minutes until batter thickens.

5. Section into 4 pieces and hand roll into spheres.

6. Serve immediately and enjoy!

Chai Bites

Total Prep and Cooking Time: 15 minutes

Makes: 8 Bites

Protein: 0g

Carbohydrates: 0g

Fat: 9g

Sodium: 1g

Fiber: 0g

Calories: 77

What you need:

- 4 tea bags chai or spiced blend

- 2 tbsp. almond butter, unsalted and softened

- 4 tbsp. coconut oil

- ⅛ cup coconut butter, softened

Steps:

1. Use small foil-lined cupcake cups and arrange on a small flat sheet.

2. Dissolve coconut butter, almond butter, and coconut oil in a saucepan, mixing occasionally until incorporated.

3. Distribute the mixture evenly to the cupcake cups and freeze for one hour.

4. Remove approximately 10 minutes before serving and enjoy!

 * *Leftovers can be stored in a freezer-safe container or Ziploc bag and will keep fresh for up to 3 months.*

Chocolate Bark

Total Prep and Cooking Time: 30 minutes

Makes: 8 Helpings

Protein: 1g

Carbohydrates: 5g

Fat: 9g

Sodium: 40g

Fiber: 1g

Calories: 95

What you need:

- ⅛ cup coconut, dried and unsweetened
- ⅛ cup hazelnuts, raw
- ⅛ cup almonds, raw
- ¼ cup coconut oil
- ⅛ cup pure maple syrup
- ⅛ tsp. iodized salt
- ¼ cup cocoa powder, sifted and unsweetened

Steps:

1. Adjust your oven to 300°F. Prepare a flat sheet with a layer of baking paper and set aside.

2. On a separate flat sheet, empty almonds and hazelnuts and heat for 6 minutes.

3. Remove the pan; spread coconut over the nuts and warm for an additional 3 minutes.

4. Use a saucepan on the lowest heat setting to dissolve coconut oil. Turn the burner off.

5. Blend maple syrup, cacao powder, roasted nuts, roasted coconut, and salt until smooth.

6. Spread the mixture out on the prepped sheet to your desired thickness.

7. Transfer to the freezer for 15 minutes until solid. Break into sections.

8. Enjoy immediately and store the leftovers in the freezer in a Ziploc freezer bag.

Chocolate Fudge Bars

Total Prep and Cooking Time: 20 minutes

Makes: 8 Bars

Protein: 6g

Carbohydrates: 16g

Fat: 15g

Sodium: 101g

Fiber: 3g

Calories: 221

What you need:

- 12 oz. dairy-free dark chocolate chips, unsweetened

- ¾ cup peanut butter, natural and no sugar added

Steps:

1. Cover an 8-square inch pan with baking lining and set aside.

2. Heat a saucepan to melt chocolate chips until liquefied. Toss the chocolate constantly, so it will not stick and burn.

3. Blend in peanut butter until the batter is smooth.

4. Distribute to the prepared pan and level out with a rubber spatula.

5. Put the fudge into the freezer for 10 minutes to firm.

6. Slice and enjoy!

Chocolate Mousse

Total Prep and Cooking Time: 15 minutes

Makes: 4 Helpings

Protein: 3g

Carbohydrates: 19g

Fat: 22g

Sodium: 31g

Fiber: 1g

Calories: 265

What you need:

- 14 oz. canned coconut milk, refrigerated

- ⅓ cup dairy-free dark chocolate

Steps:

1. Empty macadamia nuts into a glass dish the night before you prepare the cheesecake.

2. Open a can of coconut milk from the base and empty fluid into another container. Then, set aside.

3. Distribute solid coconut milk into a glass dish.

4. Use an electric beater to whip coconut milk until fluffy.

5. Transfer chocolate into a microwave-safe dish along with 4 tablespoons of liquid coconut milk.

6. Heat for 10 seconds and stir. Repeat until liquefied.

7. Fold chocolate into the fluffed coconut milk.

8. Distribute evenly between 4 ramekins or serving dishes and enjoy immediately. Alternatively, you can cover it with a section of plastic wrap until ready to serve.

Chocolate Mug Cake

Total Prep and Cooking Time:
10 minutes

Makes: 4 Helpings

Protein: 5g

Carbohydrates: 22g

Fat: 18g

Sodium: 25g

Fiber: 4g

Calories: 338

What you need:

- 4 tbsp. desiccated coconut, unsweetened and separated

- ½ cup almond flour, separated*

- 4 tbsp. brown sugar, separated

- 2⅔ tbsp. cocoa powder, unsweetened and separated

- ½ tsp. gluten-free baking powder, separated

- 4 tbsp. extra virgin olive oil, separated

- ½ cup almond milk, unsweetened and separated

- 4 tbsp. walnuts, raw, chopped and separated

Steps:

1. Set out 4 mugs and distribute 1 tablespoon of brown sugar, walnuts, and coconut to each.

2. Blend ⅛ cup of almond flour to each mug and ⅛ teaspoon of baking powder.

3. Distribute 1 tablespoon of olive oil to each mug and ⅛ cup of almond milk to each.

4. Add 2 teaspoons each of cocoa powder to the mugs.

5. Toss to fully integrate the mixture.

6. Nuke in the microwave one mug at a time for 60 seconds each.

7. Remove the mug to check if a toothpick comes out clean from the middle of the cake. If not, continue to nuke for an additional 15 seconds until successful.

8. Enjoy immediately!

* You can also substitute homemade gluten-free flour with the recipe found in chapter 13.

Coconut Mounds

Total Prep and Cooking Time:
30 minutes

Makes: 4 Helpings

Protein: 5g

Carbohydrates: 27g

Fat: 25g

Sodium: 20g

Fiber: 6g

Calories: 437

What you need:

- 1 cup desiccated coconut, unsweetened

- 7 oz. canned coconut milk, chilled

- 1 tbsp. pure maple syrup

- ½ tsp. pure vanilla extract, sugar-free

- ¾ cup dairy-free dark chocolate, chopped

Steps:

1. Prepare a flat sheet with a layer of baking paper. Set aside.

2. Open coconut milk and empty liquid portion into a container to be used at a later time in a different recipe.

3. Use a food blender to pulse vanilla extract, maple syrup, and solid coconut milk for half a minute until incorporated.

4. Mold the mixture into individual mounds either in bars or bites. You should have 8 bars or 16 bites.

5. Arrange on the prepped flat sheet leaving approximately 1 inch in between.

6. Freeze for approximately 20 minutes.

7. Just before the bars are set, chop the chocolate into small chunks and place in a small microwave-safe dish.

8. Nuke at 30 seconds increments while stirring in between until the chocolate has been liquified.

9. Remove bars from the freezer and immerse each into the chocolate, then replace them back onto the flat sheet.

10. Drizzle the remaining chocolate over bars and wait 5 minutes before serving. Enjoy!

* Store in the refrigerator for up to 7 days or in the freezer for up to 3 months.

Cookie in a Mug

Total Prep and Cooking Time: 10 minutes

Makes: 4 Helpings

Protein: 8g

Carbohydrates: 39g

Fat: 13g

Sodium: 230g

Fiber: 4g

Calories: 299

What you need:

- 3 tbsp. almond flour*
- ¼ cup brown sugar, packed
- 2 medium bananas, mashed
- ⅛ tsp. iodized salt
- 6 tbsp. peanut butter, natural and no sugar added
- 2 tsp. pure vanilla extract, sugar-free
- ½ tsp. gluten-free baking powder
- 2 tbsp. dairy free dark chocolate, chopped and separated

183

Steps:

1. Use a glass dish to combine baking powder, vanilla extract, peanut butter, salt, bananas, brown sugar, and almond flour until integrated.

2. Evenly distribute the batter to 4 mugs.

3. Fold in ½ tablespoon of dark chocolate into each mug and combine well.

4. Nuke each mug individually in the microwave for 60 seconds each.

5. A toothpick should come out of the middle relatively clean. If not, continue to nuke for 15 seconds more until successful.

6. Enjoy immediately!

   * You can also substitute homemade gluten-free flour with the recipe found in chapter 13.

Cranberry Oat Balls

Total Prep and Cooking Time:
10 minutes

Makes: 4 Balls

Protein: 4g

Carbohydrates: 15g

Fat: 5g

Sodium: 51g

Fiber: 2g

Calories: 109

What you need:

- ⅛ cup peanut butter, natural and no sugar added

- ⅓ cup gluten-free rolled oats

- ⅛ cup dried cranberries, no sugar added

- ⅔ tbsp. dairy-free dark chocolate, chopped

- 1 tbsp. pure maple syrup

- ⅛ cup quinoa, puffed

Steps:

1. Empty oats into a food blender and pulse until powdered.

2. Combine maple syrup, peanut butter, and cranberries, and continue to pulse until a thick batter starts to form.

3. Blend chocolate chips and puffed quinoa into a blender and fully integrate.

4. Divide batter into 4 sections and roll into balls with your hands.

5. Arrange on a serving platter and enjoy immediately!

Kale Chips

Total Prep and Cooking Time: 20 minutes

Makes: 4 Helpings

Protein: 0g

Carbohydrates: 1g

Fat: 5g

Sodium: 148g

Fiber: 0g

Calories: 49

What you need:

- 2 cups kale leaves

- 1½ tbsp. garlic-infused olive oil*

- ¼ tsp. iodized salt

Steps:

1. Adjust your oven to 350°F. Prepare a flat sheet with a layer of baking paper and set aside.

2. Rinse kale and discard the tough end of the stems.

3. Chop kale into bite-sized pieces and transfer to a large dish.

4. Toss with garlic-infused olive oil to coat fully. Do not drench the leaves.

5. Sprinkle with salt.

6. Arrange on the prepped flat sheet in a single layer and heat for 8 minutes. Then, carefully turn them over. Warm for an additional 5 minutes while checking regularly.

7. If you want them extra crispy, heat for another 2 minutes. Be sure they do not burn.

8. When your desired crispiness, carefully remove the pan from the oven and move to a burn-resistant area.

9. Transfer the kale chips to a serving plate and store the leftovers in a lidded container on the countertop. They will keep for up to 5 days.

* You can make your own homemade version with the recipe found in chapter 13.

Mini Key Lime Cheesecake

Total Prep and Cooking Time:
25 minutes

Makes: 4 Cheesecakes

Protein: 3g

Carbohydrates: 21g

Fat: 37g

Sodium: 179g

Fiber: 3g

Calories: 172

What you need:

- ¼ cup lime juice

- 1 small banana

- ¼ tsp. iodized salt

- 1½ cups macadamia nuts, raw and soaked overnight

- ¼ cup almond milk, unsweetened

- 3¼ tbsp. pure maple syrup, separated

- ⅓ tsp. pure vanilla extract, sugar-free

- 3¼ tbsp. coconut oil, separated

Steps:

1. Empty macadamia nuts into a glass dish the night before you prepare the cheesecake.

2. Remove water from the nuts and transfer ½ a cup to a food blender. Pulse for approximately 60 seconds or until they are a slightly chunky consistency.

3. Combine ¾ tablespoons of coconut oil and maple syrup, along with vanilla extract, salt, and banana. Pulse until the mix becomes a sticky consistency.

4. Transfer the mixture evenly between 4 quiche, pie, or ramekin dishes. Press to create a smooth surface consistently through the pans, then place in the freezer.

5. In the meantime, transfer the leftover macadamia nuts, coconut oil, and maple syrup in a food blender.

6. Blend almond milk and lime juice by pulsing for approximately 45 seconds or until a smooth consistency.

7. Transfer the pie dishes to the countertop and evenly distribute the filling between each. Use a rubber scraper to flatten the filling and create a smooth top.

8. Place the cheesecakes back into the freezer and wait approximately 1 hour or until firm before serving.

9. When ready to serve, take the cheesecakes out of the freezer 10 minutes before enjoying.

Mint Mocha Bites

Total Prep and Cooking Time: 20 minutes

Makes: 8 Bites

Protein: 1g

Carbohydrates: 24g

Fat: 7g

Sodium: 31g

Fiber: 0g

Calories: 78

What you need:

- 1 tbsp. cocoa, unsweetened and powdered, separated
- 4 tbsp. coconut oil, melted
- 1 tsp. instant coffee*
- ⅓ cup Stevia sweetener, granulated and separated
- 2 tsp. hot water
- ⅓ cup almond flour**
- ¼ tsp. pure mint extract, sugar-free

Steps:

1. Empty water into a mug and nuke in the microwave for 30 seconds.

2. Dissolve instant coffee in the hot water.

3. Using a food blender, pulse 4 tablespoons of the Stevia, 1 teaspoon of cocoa powder, 4 tablespoons of coconut oil, and ¼ teaspoon of mint extract until thoroughly combined.

4. Integrate coffee and almond flour until batter thickens.

5. Freeze for approximately 10 minutes.

6. Meanwhile, in a separate glass dish, blend the leftover 4 teaspoons of Stevia and 2 teaspoons of cocoa powder until incorporated.

7. Remove the dish from the freezer and roll into four individual balls.

8. Rotate each ball to coat it completely with the cocoa/Stevia coating and serve immediately.

9. For any leftovers, transfer to the refrigerator in a sealed tub and they will keep fresh for about 5 days.

* If you choose, you can also use decaffeinated coffee.

** You can also substitute homemade gluten-free flour with the recipe found in chapter 13.

Molasses Cookies

Total Prep and Cooking Time:
20 minutes

Makes: 8 Cookies

Protein: 0g

Carbohydrates: 17g

Fat: 8g

Sodium: 150g

Fiber: 0g

Calories: 107

What you need:

- ¼ cup brown sugar, packed

- ⅛ cup molasses

- ⅓ cup almond butter, unsalted and softened

- 1 tsp. coconut milk, liquid

- ⅓ tsp. pure vanilla extract, sugar-free

- ¾ cups almond flour*

- ⅓ tsp. ground cinnamon

- ⅛ tsp. iodized salt

- ⅔ tsp. gluten-free baking soda

- ⅓ tsp. ground ginger

- 2 tbsp. Stevia sweetener, granulated

Steps:

1. Set the temperature of your oven to 325°F and set aside a flat sheet covered with baking paper.

2. Combine almond flour, cinnamon, ginger, brown sugar, salt, baking soda, and vanilla extract in a glass dish and whisk to remove all lumpiness.

3. Pulse almond butter in a food blender for approximately 45 seconds. Blend coconut milk and molasses and integrate for another 30 seconds.

4. Finally, incorporate the flour mix slowly until fully blended.

5. Empty Stevia on a plate.

6. Divide the batter evenly and roll into 8 balls.

7. Rotate the balls in sugar to coat fully.

8. Arrange on the prepped sheet, leaving about 2 inches in between.

9. Slightly press upon each to flatten out more. The cookies will probably touch during this stage.

10. Heat for approximately 8 minutes and transfer to the stove top.

11. Wait about 5 minutes before serving. Enjoy!

 * *You can also substitute the homemade gluten-free flour with the recipe found in chapter 13.*

Muesli Bars

Total Prep and Cooking Time: 30 minutes

Makes: 8 Bars

Protein: 5g

Carbohydrates: 19g

Fat: 17g

Sodium: 19g

Fiber: 2g

Calories: 229

What you need:

- ¼ cup sunflower seeds

- ½ cup gluten-free rolled oats

- ¼ cup pumpkin seeds, raw and unsalted

- ½ tbsp flax seeds

- ¼ cup sesame seeds

- ½ cup desiccated coconut, unsweetened

- ¼ cup almond butter, unsalted

- ½ tsp. ground cinnamon

- ¼ cup pure maple syrup

Steps:

1. Prepare an 8-inch square pan with a layer of baking paper. Set aside.

2. Use a saucepan to heat cinnamon, maple syrup, and almond butter until liquefied.

3. In the meantime, transfer coconut, oats, sunflower, pumpkin, flax, and sesame seeds in a skillet. Toss occasionally for 5 minutes and turn the burner off.

4. Empty seeds into the saucepan and toss to integrate fully.

5. Transfer mix to the prepared pan and even the surface with the back of a spoon or rubber spatula.

6. Freeze for about 20 minutes or until set.

7. Slice and enjoy immediately!

Leftovers can be left in a freezer-safe container or Ziploc bag in the freezer for 1 month.

Oat Bars

Total Prep and Cooking Time: 25 minutes

Makes: 8 Bars

Protein: 2g

Carbohydrates: 14g

Fat: 1g

Sodium: 78g

Fiber: 2g

Calories: 57

What you need:

- ⅔ cup gluten-free rolled oats
- ¼ tsp. iodized salt
- ⅔ cup almond flour**
- 1 medium-ripe banana, mashed
- ⅔ tsp. ground cinnamon
- 3 tbsp. pure maple syrup
- 1 tsp. gluten-free baking powder
- ¼ cup almond milk, unsweetened

197

Steps:

1. Adjust your oven to 350°F. Set a glass baking dish layered with baking lining to the side.

2. Use a food blender to combine oats, salt, almond flour, banana, cinnamon, maple syrup, baking powder, and almond milk for approximately 2 minutes as the mixture thickens.

3. If you would like to add in fruits or nuts, do so at this time.

4. Press the mix evenly in the base of the prepared dish.

5. Heat for approximately 20 minutes, then transfer to the stove top.

6. Wait about 10 minutes before slicing and serving. Enjoy!

 Individually wrap the leftover bars in plastic wrap and store in a lidded container or plastic bag. They will keep fresh for a week on the countertop.

 **You can also substitute homemade gluten-free flour with the recipe found in chapter 13.*

Peanut Butter and Banana Granola

Total Prep and Cooking Time:
30 minutes

Makes: 4 Helpings

Protein: 9g

Carbohydrates: 29g

Fat: 16g

Sodium: 129g

Fiber: 6g

Calories: 245

What you need:

- ⅛ cup coconut oil

- ⅔ tbsp. pure maple syrup

- ⅛ cup peanut butter, natural and no sugar added

- 1 medium banana

- ⅛ tsp. iodized salt

- 1 cup gluten-free rolled oats

- ⅛ cup pumpkin seeds, raw and unsalted

- ⅛ cup sunflower seeds, raw and unsalted

Steps:

1. Set your oven to 375°F. Prepare a flat sheet with a rim with a layer of baking paper and set to the side.

2. Warm salt, maple syrup, and coconut oil in a saucepan.

3. Use a glass dish to blend sunflower and pumpkin seeds, along with oats until incorporated. Set aside.

4. In a separate dish, mash the banana with a potato masher or back of a spoon.

5. Turn the burner off for the saucepan and immediately blend the banana and peanut butter to the saucepan. Toss until consistency is relatively smooth.

6. Distribute wet mix into the oats dish and toss to combine completely.

7. Transfer the mix to the prepared flat sheet and use a rubber spatula or back of a spoon to spread it evenly across the pan.

8. Warm in the oven for approximately 22 minutes before removing to the stove top.

9. Serve immediately and enjoy!

Peanut Butter Balls

Total Prep and Cooking Time: 5 minutes

Makes: 4 Helpings

Protein: 4g

Carbohydrates: 10g

Fat: 8g

Sodium: 3g

Fiber: 2g

Calories: 108

What you need:

- ⅛ cup sunflower seeds, raw and unsalted

- ¼ tsp. flaxseed, ground

- ⅛ cup shredded coconut, unsweetened

- ¼ cup gluten-free rolled oats

- ⅛ cup peanut butter, natural and no sugar added

- ¾ tbsp. pure maple syrup

- ⅛ tsp. pure vanilla extract, sugar-free

Steps:

1. Using a food blender, integrate sunflower seeds, flaxseed, coconut, oats, peanut butter, vanilla extract, and maple syrup for approximately 2 minutes until batter becomes thick.

2. Section dough into 4 balls and roll by hand. Arrange on a serving plate and enjoy!

Peanut Butter Cookies

Total Prep and Cooking Time:
20 minutes

Makes: 8 Cookies

Protein: 5g

Carbohydrates: 24g

Fat: 6g

Sodium: 97g

Fiber: 1g

Calories: 107

What you need:

- ½ cup peanut butter, natural and no sugar added

- 1 medium banana

- ½ cup Stevia sweetener, confectioners

- ½ tsp. pure vanilla extract, sugar-free

Steps:

1. Set your oven to 350°F. Layer a flat sheet with baking paper and set aside.

2. In a glass dish, blend the banana, Stevia, peanut butter, and vanilla extract with a large rubber spatula.

3. Scoop out 1½ tablespoons of dough with a spoon and roll into small balls. Place them on the prepared cookie sheet.

4. Press dough with a fork, first horizontally, and then vertically to create a crisscross pattern.

5. Heat in the oven for approximately 14 minutes or until the edges have turned brown.

6. Transfer the flat sheet to the counter.

7. Wait 10 minutes to serve and enjoy!

Pumpkin Peanut Pudding

Total Prep and Cooking Time:
15 minutes

Makes: 4 Helpings

Protein: 6g

Carbohydrates: 18g

Fat: 15g

Sodium: 91g

Fiber: 2g

Calories: 212

What you need:

- ⅛ tsp. ground nutmeg

- ½ cup peanuts, raw and unsalted

- ⅛ tsp. iodized salt

- ⅓ cup pumpkin puree

- ¼ tsp. ground cinnamon

- ⅛ cup pure maple syrup

- ¼ cup almond milk, unsweetened

- ½ tbsp. coconut oil, melted

- ⅛ ground cloves

Steps:

1. Pulse nutmeg, peanuts, salt, pumpkin puree, cinnamon, maple syrup, almond milk, coconut oil, and cloves for approximately 3 minutes.

2. Make sure all ingredients are incorporated.

3. Divide equally into individual glasses or a dish. Serve immediately and enjoy!

Rice Pudding

Total Prep and Cooking Time: 25 minutes

Makes: 4 Helpings

Protein: 11g

Carbohydrates: 42g

Fat: 6g

Sodium: 128g

Fiber: 1g

Calories: 263

What you need:

- 4⅓ cups almond milk, unsweetened

- 3½ oz. brown rice

- 1 tbsp. brown sugar, packed

- 2 tbsp. pure maple syrup, separated

Steps:

1. Empty milk in a saucepan on the highest heat setting.

2. As it starts to bubble, turn heat to medium/low, then transfer rice into the pot. Toss to cover the rice completely.

3. Blend sugar and integrate fully. Toss frequently for 20 minutes or until it reaches the desired thickness.

4. Transfer to serving dishes and drizzle with ½ tablespoon each with maple syrup.

If the pudding thickens too quickly, you can add more almond milk until the rice is properly cooked.

Roasted Almonds

Total Prep and Cooking Time:
10 minutes

Makes: 4 Helpings

Protein: 0g

Carbohydrates: 0g

Fat: 2g

Sodium: 291g

Fiber: 0g

Calories: 17

What you need:

- ½ tsp. cumin seasoning

- ½ cup almonds, raw and unsalted

- 1½ tsp. coconut oil

- ½ tsp. iodized salt

Steps:

1. Heat a saucepan and combine cumin, almonds, coconut oil, and salt for approximately 7 minutes while stirring intermittently.

2. Remove from heat and wait approximately 5 minutes before serving.

You can substitute walnuts or pecans in this recipe.

Sweet Potato Fries

Total Prep and Cooking Time: 35 minutes

Makes: 4 Helpings

Protein: 2g

Carbohydrates: 19g

Fat: 7g

Sodium: 614g

Fiber: 3g

Calories: 143

What you need:

- 2 large sweet potatoes

- 1 tsp. iodized salt

- 2 tsp. oregano seasoning

- 1 tsp. thyme seasoning

- 2 tbsp. garlic-infused olive oil, separated*

- ½ tsp. black pepper

Steps:

1. Adjust your oven to heat at 425°F. Prepare two flat sheets with rims with 1 tablespoon each of garlic-infused olive oil. Set aside.

2. Scrub sweet potatoes thoroughly and slice into small, thin

sections with the skins still on.

3. Arrange fries evenly and in one layer between the two prepped flat sheets.

4. Drizzle with the leftover 2 tablespoons of garlic-infused olive oil.

5. Dust evenly with salt, oregano, thyme, and black pepper.

6. Heat for 15 minutes and then flip over. Heat for an additional 10 minutes or until your desired crispiness while looking for edges to turn dark brown. Once they do, you know they are done.

7. Remove from the oven and enjoy immediately with your favorite sauce.

 * *You can make your own homemade version with the recipe found in chapter 13.*

 ** *There are a variety of sauces and dips that you can make at home found in chapter 13.*

Vanilla Cinnamon Bites

Total Prep and Cooking Time: 30 minutes

Makes: 8 Helpings

Protein: 1g

Carbohydrates: 8g

Fat: 3g

Sodium: 2g

Fiber: 2g

Calories: 55

What you need:

- ⅓ cup gluten-free rolled oats

- ¼ cup almond flour*

- 2½ tbsp. ground cinnamon, separated

- ⅛ cup almond butter, unsalted

- ½ tsp pure vanilla extract, sugar-free

- ⅛ cup pure maple syrup

Steps:

1. Set aside a flat sheet layered with baking lining.

2. Empty oats into a food blender and pulse until powdered. Then, transfer to a glass dish.

3. Blend vanilla extract, maple syrup, almond flour, and butter, as well as 1½ tablespoons of cinnamon until incorporated.

4. Your batter should be slightly sticky and holding together. If it is too dry, add another tablespoon of maple syrup.

5. Divide batter into 8 equal sections and create spheres out of each.

6. Arrange on the prepped flat sheet and place in the freezer for 20 minutes.

7. Empty the leftover tablespoon of cinnamon onto a plate.

8. Remove the tray from the freezer and roll each ball in cinnamon, so they are fully coated.

9. Enjoy immediately, or you can store it in the fridge for up to a month. Store in a Ziploc bag to ensure freshness.

You can also substitute homemade gluten-free flour with the recipe found in chapter 13.

Chapter Thirteen:
Sauce, Dressing and Essential Ingredient Recipes

Apple Cider Vinaigrette

Total Prep and Cooking Time: 5 minutes

Makes: 8 Helpings

Protein: 0g

Carbohydrates: 0g

Fat: 3g

Sodium: 39g

Fiber: 0g

Calories: 32

What you need:

- ⅛ tsp. iodized salt
- ¼ cup garlic-infused olive oil*
- ⅛ cup apple cider vinegar
- ⅓ tsp. brown sugar, packed
- ⅛ tsp. black pepper

Steps:

1. Empty salt, garlic-infused olive oil, apple cider vinegar, sugar, and black pepper into a glass jar with a lid.

2. Enclose with the lid tightly and shake to integrate fully.

3. Keep in a cool, dry place. It should stay good for up to 4 weeks.

* You can make your own homemade version with the recipe found in chapter 13.

Basil Vinaigrette

Total Prep and Cooking Time:
5 minutes

Makes: 8 Helpings

Protein: 0g

Carbohydrates: 0g

Fat: 7g

Sodium: 39g

Fiber: 0g

Calories: 60

What you need:

- 1 cup basil leaves

- 1⅓ tbsp. lemon juice

- ⅛ tsp. iodized salt

- ¼ cup extra virgin olive oil

Steps:

1. Use a food blender to pulse basil, olive oil, lemon juice, and salt until the basil is finely chopped.

2. Store in a lidded container in the refrigerator until ready to use. It will keep for up to 6 months.

Chicken Stock

Total Prep and Cooking Time: 35 minutes

Makes: 2½ cups

Protein: 2g

Carbohydrates: 2g

Fat: 1g

Sodium: 528g

Fiber: 0g

Calories: 24

What you need:

- Bones from 2 chickens
- Tap water

Steps:

1. Place chicken bones in a pressure cooker.

2. Cover with water so the bones are covered by 2 inches.

3. Pressurize for 30 minutes, then use a colander to transfer the broth into a large dish with a spout.

4. Use cheesecloth to remove any smaller debris from the broth as you transfer to a large lidded glass container.

Chive Pesto Sauce

Total Prep and Cooking Time: 10 minutes

Makes: 8 Helpings

Protein: 2g

Carbohydrates: 2g

Fat: 19g

Sodium: 102g

Fiber: 0g

Calories: 186

What you need:

- ½ cup extra virgin olive oil
- ⅛ cup chives, chopped
- ¼ tsp. iodized salt
- ½ cup basil leaves
- ¼ cup Parmesan cheese, grated
- ½ cup pine nuts
- 1 tsp. lemon juice
- ¼ tsp. black pepper

Steps:

1. Use a food blender to pulse olive oil, chives, basil, Parmesan cheese, pine nuts, and lemon juice until your desired consistency.

2. Blend black pepper and salt, then store in a lidded container in the refrigerator until needed. It will keep for up to 3 months.

Garlic Infused Olive Oil

Total Prep and Cooking Time:
10 minutes + 2 hours infusing

Makes: 2 cups

Protein: 0g

Carbohydrates: 0g

Fat: 6g

Sodium: 116g

Fiber: 0g

Calories: 53

What you need:

- 2 cups extra virgin olive oil

- 6 cloves garlic, peeled and halved

Steps:

1. Peel garlic cloves and slice into halves. Set aside.

2. Empty oil in a saucepan and warm at the lowest heat setting.

3. When oil is warm to touch, turn the burner off.

4. Transfer garlic to the oil and allow to sit for 2 hours.

5. Use a cheesecloth to separate garlic from the oil.

6. You can store it in a lidded glass jar for up to 3 days or freeze in an ice cube tray and use it for over three months' time.

Guacamole Dip

Total Prep and Cooking Time:
10 minutes

Makes: 2 Smoothies

Protein: 1g

Carbohydrates: 5g

Fat: 8g

Sodium: 84g

Fiber: 3g

Calories: 90

What you need:

- ⅛ tsp. iodized salt

- 1 tbsp. coconut milk, chilled

- ⅛ cup spinach leaves, chopped

- ⅔ tsp. garlic-infused olive oil*

- 1 cup avocado, chopped

- ⅔ tbsp. coriander leaves, chopped

- ⅓ tbsp. lime juice

- ⅛ tsp black pepper

Steps:

1. Slice avocado in half and discard the seed. Roughly chop into smaller sections and set aside.

2. Rinse spinach and coriander leaves, then shake to remove any excess moisture. Chop roughly.

3. Open the canned coconut milk and empty the liquid into a lidded container to be used with another recipe at a later time.

4. Use a food blender to pulse black pepper, lime juice, garlic-infused olive oil, coriander, spinach, avocado, and coconut milk for approximately 90 seconds or until it is your desired consistency.

5. Transfer to a serving dish and enjoy immediately!

* You can make your own homemade version with the recipe found in chapter 13.

** You can also store it in the fridge in a serving dish with a layer of plastic wrap enclosing the dip. It will keep for up to 3 days.

Homemade Gluten-Free Flour

Total Prep and Cooking Time:
15 minutes

Makes: 5 pounds

Protein: 2g

Carbohydrates: 22g

Fat: 1g

Sodium: 4g

Fiber: 1g

Calories: 103

What you need:

- 2¾ cups millet flour
- 2½ cups white rice flour
- 1⅔ cup brown rice flour
- 2¾ cups sorghum flour
- 1⅔ cup buckwheat flour
- 2½ cups potato starch
- 1⅔ cup arrowroot flour

Steps:

1. Use a large glass dish to sift millet, white rice, brown rice, sorghum, buckwheat, arrowroot flours, and potato starch.

2. Whisk flour together so it is fully integrated.

3. Transfer to a large lidded container and store in a cool place. It will keep up to one year.

Lemon Dill Pesto

Total Prep and Cooking Time: 5 minutes

Makes: 8 Helpings

Protein: 0g

Carbohydrates: 0g

Fat: 7g

Sodium: 147g

Fiber: 0g

Calories: 62

What you need:

- ½ tsp. iodized salt
- 2 cups dill, loosely packed
- ¼ cup extra virgin olive oil
- ⅛ sp. black pepper
- 2 tbsp. lemon juice

Steps:

1. Use a food blender to pulse dill, olive oil, salt, lemon juice, and black pepper until it has a slightly chunky consistency.

2. Store in a lidded container in the refrigerator until ready to use. It will keep for up to 3 months.

Lemon Pepper Seasoning

Total Prep and Cooking Time: 25 minutes

Makes: 4 Tablespoons

Protein: 0g

Carbohydrates: 1g

Fat: 0g

Sodium: 194g

Fiber: 0g

Calories: 2

What you need:

- 1 tsp. iodized salt

- Zest from 4-5 lemons

- 1½ tbsp. black pepper

Steps:

1. Set your oven to 250°F.

2. Prepare a flat sheet with a layer of tin foil.

3. Spread lemon zest and black pepper over the sheet and warm for 18 minutes.

4. Toss salt into the mixture and store it in a lidded container in a dark area. It will keep for up to 3 months.

Maple Mustard Sauce

Total Prep and Cooking Time: 5 minutes

Makes: 8 Helpings

Protein: 1g

Carbohydrates: 20g

Fat: 4g

Sodium: 303g

Fiber: 1g

Calories: 113

What you need:

- ⅔ cup pure maple syrup

- ¼ cup extra virgin olive oil

- ⅔ cup Dijon mustard

Steps:

1. Use a glass dish to blend maple syrup, olive oil, and Dijon mustard until consistency is smooth.

2. Store in a lidded container in the refrigerator. It will keep for up to three months.

Raspberry Rhubarb Compote

Total Prep and Cooking Time:
15 minutes

Makes: 8 Helpings

Protein: 0g

Carbohydrates: 11g

Fat: 0g

Sodium: 1g

Fiber: 1g

Calories: 18

What you need:

- ¼ cup rhubarb

- ⅛ cup water

- Zest of 1 lime

- ⅛ cup Stevia sweetener, granulated

- 1 tbsp. lime juice

- ¼ cup raspberries

- 1⅓ tsp. chia seeds

Steps:

1. Rinse rhubarb and allow it to drain properly in a colander.

2. Chop the rhubarb into smaller sections and transfer to a saucepan. Heat at medium/high setting.

3. Blend lime juice, zest, Stevia, and water. Toss to blend fully.

4. Allow mixture to bubble, then turn the burner to the lowest heat setting.

5. Enclose the pan and heat for an additional 5 minutes or until the rhubarb has softened.

6. Transfer raspberries to the saucepan and heat for approximately 3 minutes or until they become mushy.

7. Turn the burner off and toss in chia seeds until completely incorporated.

8. Allow to cool if transferring to a plastic container. If using a glass container, transfer immediately.

9. Set in the refrigerator and use it within 7 days.

Rosemary Butter

Total Prep and Cooking Time: 5 minutes

Makes: 8 Helpings

Protein: 0g

Carbohydrates: 0g

Fat: 14g

Sodium: 43g

Fiber: 0g

Calories: 122

What you need:

- 4 tsp. fresh rosemary, chopped

- ½ cup coconut butter, unsalted and softened

- 4 tsp. capers, chopped

- 4 tsp. garlic-infused olive oil*

Steps:

1. Use a glass dish to combine rosemary, coconut butter, capers, and garlic-infused olive oil until a smooth consistency.

2. Spoon onto a lidded container and place in the refrigerator until ready to use.

* You can make your own homemade version with the recipe found in chapter 13.

Teriyaki Sauce

Total Prep and Cooking Time: 10 minutes

Makes: 8 Helpings

Protein: 2g

Carbohydrates: 15g

Fat: 2g

Sodium: 53g

Fiber: 0g

Calories: 83

What you need:

- ½ cup pure maple syrup
- 1 tbsp. garlic-infused olive oil*
- ½ cup tamari, low sodium
- 4 inches ginger, shredded

Steps:

1. Use a food blender to pulse ginger, garlic-infused olive oil, tamari, and maple syrup for approximately 30 seconds or until a smooth consistency.

2. Refrigerate any leftovers in a lidded container and use within 3 months.

* You can make your own homemade version with the recipe found in chapter 13.

Thousand Island Dressing

Total Prep and Cooking Time: 5 minutes

Makes: 8 Helpings

Protein: 0g

Carbohydrates: 0g

Fat: 6g

Sodium: 174g

Fiber: 0g

Calories: 54

What you need:

- ½ cup extra virgin olive oil, separated

- 2 tsp. gluten-free Worcestershire sauce

- 1 tsp. lemon juice

Steps:

1. Blend lemon juice, Worcestershire sauce, and olive oil until incorporated.

2. Transfer to a lidded container and it will keep up to one month in the refrigerator. Enjoy!

Vegetable Stock Powder

Total Prep and Cooking Time: 10 minutes

Makes: 8 tablespoons

Protein: 0g

Carbohydrates: 0g

Fat: 0g

Sodium: 1239g

Fiber: 0g

Calories: 4

What you need:

- ⅛ cup celery, chopped
- ⅛ cup fennel, chopped
- ⅛ cup parsley, chopped
- 1 small carrot, chopped
- ⅛ cup coriander, chopped
- ⅛ cup iodized salt

Steps:

1. Rinse celery, fennel, parsley, carrot, and coriander and shake to remove any extra moisture.

2. Chop celery and carrots into smaller sections and distribute to a food blender.

3. Pulse for approximately 90 seconds or until minced.

4. Roughly chop fennel, parsley, and coriander and transfer to a food blender with salt.

5. Continue to pulse until fully integrated and store in a lidded container or Ziploc bag.

6. For every 2 cups of broth that you require, mix with 1 tablespoon of this powder with 2 cups of boiling water and toss until dissolved.

Chapter Fourteen:
Tips and Tricks for Success

What If You Do Not See Improvement?

There are approximately 30% of people whose symptoms of IBS will not decrease while following this diet.[17] However, there are a couple of tips to try before you give up.

Pay Special Attention to Ingredient Lists

As mentioned, food companies will include additives into pre-packaged foods, often times FODMAPs. Even in small amounts, additives of xylitol, sorbitol, garlic, and onions can cause symptoms of IBS to occur.

Eliminate Stressors

When it comes to your health, food may not be the only aspect triggering your IBS symptoms. In fact, another huge component is stress. Take a hard look at what stressors that you have in your life and work to reduce or eliminate them. Even if you are following a low FODMAP diet, your symptoms will likely persist if you are still under severe stress.[18]

---

[17] Mullin, Gerard E., et al. "Irritable Bowel Syndrome: Contemporary Nutrition Management Strategies." Journal of Parenteral and Enteral Nutrition, vol. 38, no. 7, 2014, pp. 781–799., doi:10.1177/0148607114545329.

[18] Pellissier, S., and B. Bonaz. "The Place of Stress and Emotions in the Irritable Bowel Syndrome." Anxiety Vitamins and Hormones, 2017, pp. 327–354., doi:10.1016/bs.vh.2016.09.005.

Keep Up to Date

There are many new tests being done of FODMAP foods, and the lists are updating regularly. This is also why there are various contradicting lists on the internet. Instead, download the app for Monash University or keep checking their website for updates on the latest in research and knowledge.

Take Away Temptation

While you are in the first two phases of this diet, it is important to remove any high FODMAP foods in your pantry, fridge, and freezer if at all possible. If your family is not following this diet, pay special attention when you are cooking your meals to keep any low and high FODMAP foods separate by using different dishes. It is also important to store any leftovers in separate containers.

Eating Out Tips

This can be especially stressful when you do not prepare yourself ahead of time. If you have a favorite restaurant that knows you well, explain to them your situation, and they will most likely accommodate your personal needs. For any restaurants you have not frequented, look online to see if they have published their menu, so you can review your meals ahead of time. Doing this allows you some time in the restaurant and doesn't force you to have to sift through the food for a long period, especially if you are with other people.

Ask the waiter if the meal you would like is cooked with high FODMAP foods like garlic and onion and request that they are not. You can also choose to go to an organic, vegan, or vegetarian restaurant, as they should be able to customize your meals to your particular needs.

Another tip is to go for a simpler meal, as there will be fewer ingredients. You can also ask for plain meats and fish, so you don't have to worry about dealing with toppings or a sauce that you are unsure about. To make things less stressful for you, opt out of restaurants with cuisines with bold flavors and rich sauces such as Indian or Chinese. A better option would be to go to an Italian or Japanese restaurant, as they will be more likely to have more simplified food options.

Of course, it does take more time to eat out and enjoy your meal at a restaurant, but with a little compromise and patience, it is doable.

It Takes Time

Be sure to give this elimination diet a chance to work. In most cases, you will see results within two months; however, for more severe cases, it can take up to six months for your symptoms to reduce significantly. Each person is different, and if you give up too quickly, you may take away your chances of living a more comfortable and healthy life.

Chapter Summary

- Even if a food is labeled or appears natural or healthy, take a closer look at the ingredients label. Doing so will determine if the manufacturing company has added high FODMAP ingredients into your prepared foods. It will also let you know if they were packaged in a facility where gluten or lactose products were also being prepared.

- Stress is also a major factor to symptoms of digestive upset. Take special care to diminish, avoid, or eliminate people, places, and situations that may cause your stress levels to rise above normal. If you find that you are unable to reduce stress, incorporate calming or breathing exercises into your daily routine to aid with stress levels.

- There are constant research studies being conducted that continue to shed light on moderate and high FODMAP foods, as well as changes in serving amounts. Be sure to keep up to date with the latest by frequenting the Monash University website or downloading their app for up-to-date information.

In the next chapter, you will learn common questions and answers for people following a low FODMAP diet.

Chapter Fifteen:
Common Questions and Answers

Can vegetarians follow a low FODMAP diet?

It is possible to do so, but it will be more difficult. The reason for a more difficult standard is that legumes, which are high in FODMAPs, are the staple protein in the vegetarian diet. As was outlined in this book, you can lower the number of legumes within your diet, keeping servings to ¼ cup. Other high protein options that vegetarians can include in their diet are seeds, nuts, eggs, tofu, tempeh, and a meat substitute known as Quorn.[19]

What if I am not seeing an improvement in my symptoms?

If you have gone through the elimination process, and you are not seeing a reduction in your symptoms, it is possible that you are still consuming hidden FODMAPs in your pre-packaged foods. It could also be because you are consuming too high a serving of moderate FODMAP foods, such as pumpkin puree, avocado, and sweet potatoes. If you are unable to pinpoint the exact reason, it would be wise to check in with your nutritionist to gain some insight into what the problem may be, whether it is due to your diet or another health concern.

---

[19] Mullin, Gerard E., et al. "Irritable Bowel Syndrome: Contemporary Nutrition Management Strategies." Journal of Parenteral and Enteral Nutrition, vol. 38, no. 7, 2014, pp. 781–799., doi:10.1177/0148607114545329.

Would you lose weight with the FODMAP diet?

No, as the focus is not weight loss; it is solely a diet that restricts high FODMAP foods, so you can avoid gastrointestinal discomfort. It is also an aid to those who suffer from IBS. In fact, if you are experiencing a noticeable amount of weight loss, it would be wise to consult your doctor to determine the cause and reevaluate whether the low FODMAP diet is right for you.

What foods have dietary fiber/fructans?

There are high amounts of these high FODMAPs in wheat, onions, garlic, leeks, asparagus, artichokes, and agave.[20]

What is FODMAP intolerance?

This is a description given to people who are suffering from the following gastrointestinal symptoms: constipation, diarrhea, bloating, gas, or a combination of these symptoms, and who are eating an excess amount of FODMAP foods. This can include high FODMAP foods, as well as higher serving amounts of moderate FODMAP foods, such as avocados.

What kind of bread can I eat on a FODMAP diet?

You can consume gluten-free white bread, sourdough bread, cornbread, and millet bread. If you are purchasing instead of making at home, be sure to read the ingredients list carefully to ensure there are no high FODMAPs included.

---

[20] "Low FODMAP Diet." Stanford Health Care (SHC) - Stanford Medical Center, 2019, https://stanfordhealthcare.org/medical-treatments/l/low-fodmap-diet.html.

My family members are not following this diet. Can I just cook their food and then remove any high FODMAP foods from my plate?

It is not wise to do this. As an example, garlic and onion are foods that your other family members can eat, but the FODMAPs that are probably triggering your symptoms will probably have been blended into the entire dish upon cooking, as FODMAPs are water soluble. Even though it can make things more difficult, it is best for your health and for this diet to work properly that you cook your meals separately.

Alternatively, you can switch your family members to the low FODMAP diet while you are in the elimination stage. It is likely they may also be experiencing the same or similar symptoms too, and you can also reassure them that this is just for a short period until you determine which foods are making you have symptoms.

Does organic matter to the level of FODMAPs?

The FODMAP levels in food are not affected by how the food was grown; however, if eating organic is important to you, by all means continue. The FODMAPs in food are determined by the amount of sugars included, along with the time of the year they are produced. If they are grown in a greenhouse off season, they will have differing amounts of FODMAPs compared to being grown naturally.

What are some common foods with hidden FODMAPs?

Since FODMAPs are generally used as a flavoring, they are found in many prepackaged and prepared foods. You need to be diligent because foods that you consider healthy, such as muesli bars, can also contain them. Make a habit to check the ingredients lists, even if the package says natural or healthy. They can even be found in certain spices such as chili powder. Use the shopping food list reference in chapter 3 and keep up to date with the Monash University website.

Do I have to follow this diet forever?

It is not recommended to follow this diet for the long term. In fact, you should be going through the process for 3 to 6 months maximum. If you find you are still having gastrointestinal problems past 3 months, consult with your licensed dietitian or medical doctor to gain more guidance. The only foods you will be eliminating from your diet for the long term are moderate and high FODMAPs that are causing your gastrointestinal symptoms to return.

Do I have to eliminate dairy foods completely?

Every individual's body is different and responds to foods differently. You do not need to cut out dairy altogether, as they have many beneficial vitamins and minerals that your body requires. However, you will be eliminating any foods with lactose, including animal and soy milk, yogurt, and hard cheeses. Instead, you can still enjoy soft cheeses, nut milks, and lactose-free yogurt with no added sweeteners.

On the other hand, these recommended dairy products do still contain a miniscule amount of lactose. If you are experiencing symptoms of dairy sensitivities, you may eliminate them during the first phase. Remember, though, that it is important to get your calcium from other sources, such as almonds and salmon.

What precautions should I have with my medications, supplements, and probiotics?

This is usually overlooked, as precautions are not usually considered by very many people. However, you will also need to check your medications and supplements to ensure that they also do not include high FODMAPs. As an example, whey protein supplements are a high FODMAP food.

You will probably be told by your licensed dietitian to avoid using probiotics while you are adjusting your diet. If you are incorporating probiotics in your regime, there is a possibility that you will not discover the high FODMAP foods that are causing your gut issues. Probiotics can also contain inulin or milk, which are not recommended for a low FODMAP diet.

Should I avoid gluten?

In this particular book, it is recommended to avoid gluten so that you can determine which high FODMAP foods are triggering your symptoms. Gluten products such as barley, rye, and wheat are high in fructans, so they make the list for restricted items. Because they are classified as such, some experts believe that you can consume them, but in very small quantities and very infrequently.

On the other hand, there are many options for gluten-free products that are also loaded with nutrients, but they can also contain high FODMAP ingredients such as inulin, honey, or milk. This is where looking at the ingredient labels for all of your foods will help you to keep on track with your diet.

Are FODMAPs affected by the cooking process?

You will find that preserved or canned foods in acidic conditions will have the highest content of FODMAPs, which, as stated earlier for other reasons, is due to FODMAPs being water soluble. While they are sitting in cans or containers, the FODMAPs will leech out into the fluid. Even removing the fluid will not remove all the high FODMAPs, as the food has been marinating in the high FODMAP brine.

Along the same lines, if you decide to use canned or preserved foods that have been drained and washed thoroughly, high temperatures these foods are being cooked in is not necessarily going to bring down the high FODMAP levels, as it varies greatly on the food, how it is cooked, and at what temperature. Because there is no clear-cut, scientific way of knowing the reaction of these foods, it is better to refrain from high FODMAP foods altogether and use fresh products when available.

Is it better to eat larger meals or smaller and more frequent meals for a low FODMAP diet?

For the most effective impact to your health, it is best to stick to three meals during the day, along with a snack in between, as needed. If you find that you are too hungry in between your meals, modify your serving sizes during your meals to be slightly larger, as long as you are not consuming too much of a moderate FODMAP food like a pumpkin puree, avocados, or sweet potatoes. You can also eat more filling snacks in between your meals, and you may find it helpful to bring this information to the attention of your licensed dietitian, and they can give you specific suggestions for what to eat to eliminate this issue.

Where can I find a specialist dietitian?

Australia

Visit this website: https://daa.asn.au/find-an-apd/ (Accredited Practicing Dietitian), which is part of the Dietitians Association of Australia. In the drop-down menu, select gastrointestinal, bowel, and stomach disorders.

Canada

Visit the website for Dietitians of Canada to find licensed nutritionists in your area:

https://members.dietitians.ca/DCMember/s/find-dietitian?language=en_US

USA

The Academy of Nutrition and Dietetics has a section to search for a registered dietitian: https://www.eatright.org/find-an-expert

UK

Search for specialized FODMAP dietitians from King's College London on their website: https://www.kcl.ac.uk/solcs

Is there any other method that can improve my absorption of FODMAPs?

Lactose (disaccharides)

You can experiment with lactase enzyme products if you have issues with lactose intolerance or malabsorption. They can be purchased as tablets or drops from pharmacies and work to break down lactose present in dairy foods. It is wise to try this method after you are in phase 3 of this diet.

Oligosaccharides

Recent research has suggested that the enzyme supplement **alpha-galactosidase (α-GAL)** has a positive effect in digesting **galacto-oligosaccharides (GOS)** found in legumes. This can be an alternative method for vegans and vegetarians who are following a low FODMAP diet, as they usually have legumes as a staple protein source in their diet.

What happens if I break this diet?

Do not fret—the main goal of following this diet is to gain more control over your symptoms and the foods that are causing them.

When you intake a food item that is high in FODMAPs, it will throw your entire process out the window; however, it is always wise to continue eliminating this food during phase 1 and 2 of the diet, then switch back to a low FODMAP diet if you are currently in phase 3 or completed with the low FODMAP diet. Doing so should reduce or eliminate the symptoms that have arisen.

Chapter Summary

- Vegans and vegetarians can follow a low FODMAP diet, though the elimination of legumes (with its being high in FODMAPs) can be a bit of a challenge. However, they can customize their diet by including only a quarter cup of legumes or using the α-GAL enzyme supplement to aid in digestion of legumes.

- If you are the only one in your family following a low FODMAP diet, it is essential to cook your foods separate from their meal. FODMAPs are water soluble and able to still appear when cooked. It is also necessary to store any leftover food in a separate container.

- Finding a specialized and certified nutritionist will help you get the most out of your low FODMAP diet. Because each body reacts to foods differently, you will benefit greatly from having personalized support. They can also help you through each phase of the diet and instruct you on a particular method of reintroducing high FODMAP foods back into your food.

In the next chapter, you will learn about additional resources that you can explore to learn more about IBS and the low FODMAP diet.

Chapter Sixteen:
Helpful Resources

A Little Bit Yummy is a website where you will find additional low FODMAP recipes, meal plans, and online courses to help educate you further on FODMAPs. You will even be able to modify your current favorite recipes, so they are low in FODMAPs and compliant to your needs. Visit the website at

https://alittlebityummy.com/

The mission of **Celiac Sprue Association (CSA)** is to provide information on celiac disease and gluten-free diets. They have workshops and conferences that they use to raise awareness about celiac disease in the local community, and they also have a listing of certified gluten-free products, which you can look at to gain guidance and count your gluten-free carbohydrates.

https://nationalceliac.org/

Crohn's & Colitis Foundation (CCFA) is an organization founded over 50 years ago, whose mission statement is to improve the quality of life and cure people who suffer from ulcerative colitis and Crohn's disease. With over 40 individual chapters throughout the United States, it is possible there is one in your area. They offer current information and research, as well as support groups for individual patients and families.

https://www.crohnscolitisfoundation.org/

Everyday Nutrition FODMAP Challenge Club is a 3-month long online program that will continue to set up challenges for you to accomplish as you push toward your goals. You will receive professional guidance from dietitians, and it features a community of supporters going through the same experiences that you are with the low FODMAP diet.

https://www.fodmapeveryday.com/everyday-nutrition-fodmap-challenge-online-program/

When you need to find out more information about your digestive disorders, **The International Foundation for Functional Gastrointestinal Disorders (IFFGD)** is an excellent resource. They offer assistance, support, and knowledge about an entire range of gastrointestinal upsets and disorders. The foundation is also set up for children along with adults. They keep their website up to date with current research and news, and you are also able to find a medical doctor in your local area through their website. Visit https://www.iffgd.org/ to find out more.

If you are having trouble getting in contact with a licensed dietitian, or you are unable to afford one, **The Low FODMAP for Beginner's Course** can put your mind at ease. It is an easy-to-follow with a daily support system, which will help guide you through the ins and outs of the low FODMAP diet, so you will find success and rid yourself of your intestinal symptoms. https://www.fodmapeveryday.com/the-low-fodmap-diet-beginners-course/

National Digestive Diseases Information Clearinghouse (NDDIC) is sponsored by the National Institute of Diabetes and Digestive and Kidney Diseases (NIDDK). They have many answers to frequently asked questions about digestive health, diseases, and nutritional information, and they also have a search to find local support grounds and digestive health doctors in your area. https://www.niddk.nih.gov/health-information/digestive-diseases

She Can't Eat What? is a blog created by Emma Hatcher, in which she creates her own low FODMAP recipes. Follow her at https://shecanteatwhat.com/

Final Words

After having read more about how you can alleviate your IBS and gastrointestinal upset symptoms, you can have hope for comfort in your future. There is a high quality of life that you can gain in a life without these diseases, and you can reduce or even cure them with the help from the low FODMAP diet method. There should now be no reason why you should delay and continue to suffer any longer.

Using the methods laid out in this book makes the process much more simplified and gives you a direction to continue with confidence. Start as soon as possible by ridding your kitchen of any high FODMAP foods, so you can start with the elimination process. Remember to create your shopping lists and continue to look for bargains on food you buy regularly.

You now also have a variety of recipes to use for starting to cook your low FODMAP foods, so you can start easing your symptoms this week. How exciting is that? Continue through the process for this short time, and you will see major changes in your attitude, lifestyle, and quality of life in a matter of months. Who knew that being rid of these debilitating symptoms could take such a short time?

Remember to be patient with yourself through the whole process. You will be getting more in touch with your body in a way that you probably have not before. It will be a learning and trial-and-error process for you. However, you now have the tools and knowledge that you need to continue forward with hope and confidence. You do not need to feel helpless any longer.

Be sure to research and find a certified nutritionist whom you can trust to take you through this journey and remember to continue to follow current and ongoing research projects, so you can work on and tweak your diet as necessary. New knowledge is being discovered through the medical studies every day, and these research studies will continue to strengthen your own knowledge of what you are experiencing. There is always an answer, so always be searching if this particular book happened to not answer all of your questions.

I am proud that you have taken this first step in helping you better your health, lifestyle, and wellbeing. It is a wonderful decision that you are not going to regret. Continue moving forward because there is nothing that should hold you back from enjoying your life to the fullest. With just a few adjustments to your diet, you will brighten your attitude and outlook on life because your focus will not solely be centered around your gastrointestinal symptoms.

Continue to work through the methods, even if you run into challenges. Find support groups and friends that will help you along the way. You are not alone, and this is nothing you should be embarrassed about. When you are more open to the information out there and the people who have gone through the same experiences, you will find that a whole new network of supporters are out there to cheer you along.

I do hope that you have gained everything that you needed and more from this book. My promise is that you will feel a difference in your body, and symptoms should have come to fruition. If you are still struggling, again, reach out. You are not going through these things alone, and there is no reason to do so. There is always a solution, so do not fret and worry. Remember that your positive attitude, diminished stress, and following a low FODMAP diet will take you into a life that you are going to enjoy.

Please take the time to share this book with your family and friends if they are suffering through gastrointestinal issues or IBS, so we can make sure that more and more people are able to live their life to the fullest, even after being diagnosed. I wish you a happy journey into your newfound life, and all the best!

Dr. Beth Ganley

Resources

1. Böhn, Lena, et al. "Diet Low in FODMAPs Reduces Symptoms of Irritable Bowel Syndrome as Well as Traditional Dietary Advice: A Randomized Controlled Trial." *Gastroenterology*, vol. 149, no. 6, 2015, doi:10.1053/j.gastro.2015.07.054.

2. "Diagnosis and Management of Irritable Bowel Syndrome in Adults in Primary Care: Summary of NICE Guidance." *Bmj*, vol. 350, no. Mar 03 16, Mar. 2015, doi:10.1136/bmj.h1216.

3. Drossman, Douglas A., and William L. Hasler. "Rome IV— Functional GI Disorders: Disorders of Gut-Brain Interaction." *Gastroenterology*, vol. 150, no. 6, 2016, pp. 1257–1261., doi:10.1053/j.gastro.2016.03.035.

4. Gearry, Richard B., et al. "Reduction of Dietary Poorly Absorbed Short-Chain Carbohydrates (FODMAPs) Improves Abdominal Symptoms in Patients with Inflammatory Bowel Disease — A Pilot Study." *Journal of Crohns and Colitis*, vol. 3, no. 1, 2009, pp. 8–14., doi:10.1016/j.crohns.2008.09.004.

5. Gibson, P. R., and S. J. Shepherd. "Personal View: Food for Thought - Western Lifestyle and Susceptibility to Crohn's Disease. The FODMAP Hypothesis." *Alimentary Pharmacology and Therapeutics*, vol. 21, no. 12, 2005, pp. 1399–1409., doi:10.1111/j.1365-2036.2005.02506.x.

6. Gibson, Peter R, and Susan J Shepherd. "Evidence-Based Dietary Management of Functional Gastrointestinal Symptoms: The FODMAP Approach." Journal of Gastroenterology and Hepatology, vol. 25, no. 2, 2010, pp. 252–258., doi:10.1111/j.1440-1746.2009.06149.x.

7. Hungin, A. P. S., et al. "Irritable Bowel Syndrome in the United States: Prevalence, Symptom Patterns and Impact." *Alimentary Pharmacology and Therapeutics*, vol. 21, no. 11, 2005, pp. 1365–1375., doi:10.1111/j.1365-2036.2005.02463.x.

8. Lis, Dana, et al. "Case Study: Utilizing a Low FODMAP Diet to Combat Exercise-Induced Gastrointestinal Symptoms." *International Journal of Sport Nutrition and Exercise Metabolism*, vol. 26, no. 5, 2016, pp. 481–487., doi:10.1123/ijsnem.2015-0293.

9. "Low FODMAP Diet." *Stanford Health Care (SHC) - Stanford Medical Center*, 2019, https://stanfordhealthcare.org/medical-treatments/l/low-fodmap-diet.html.

10. Lydiard, R. Bruce. "Gastrointestinal Disorders, Irritable Bowel Syndrome, and Anxiety." *Anxiety Disorders*, 2015, pp. 255–266., doi:10.1093/med/9780199395125.003.0018.

11. Marsh, Abigail, et al. "Does a Diet Low in FODMAPs Reduce Symptoms Associated with Functional Gastrointestinal Disorders? A Comprehensive Systematic Review and Meta-Analysis." *European Journal of Nutrition*, vol. 55, no. 3, 2015, pp. 897–906., doi:10.1007/s00394-015-0922-1.

12. Meyer, D, and M Stasse-Wolthuis. "The Bifidogenic Effect of Inulin and Oligofructose and Its Consequences for Gut Health." *European Journal of Clinical Nutrition*, vol. 63, no. 11, 2009, pp. 1277–1289., doi:10.1038/ejcn.2009.64.

13. Mullin, Gerard E., et al. "Irritable Bowel Syndrome: Contemporary Nutrition Management Strategies." *Journal of*

Parenteral and Enteral Nutrition, vol. 38, no. 7, 2014, pp. 781–799., doi:10.1177/0148607114545329.

14. Pellissier, S., and B. Bonaz. "The Place of Stress and Emotions in the Irritable Bowel Syndrome." *Anxiety Vitamins and Hormones*, 2017, pp. 327–354., doi:10.1016/bs.vh.2016.09.005.

15. Staudacher, Heidi M., et al. "Fermentable Carbohydrate Restriction Reduces Luminal Bifidobacteria and Gastrointestinal Symptoms in Patients with Irritable Bowel Syndrome." *The Journal of Nutrition*, vol. 142, no. 8, 2012, pp. 1510–1518., doi:10.3945/jn.112.159285.

Made in the USA
Monee, IL
01 September 2020